DATE			

TWAYNE'S WORLD LEADERS SERIES

John Kenneth Galbraith

John Kenneth Galbraith

John Kenneth Galbraith

JOHN S. GAMBS

TWAYNE PUBLISHERS

A DIVISION OF G. K. HALL & CO., BOSTON

Library of Congress Cataloging in Publication Data

Gambs, John Saké, 1899-
  John Kenneth Galbraith.

  (Twayne's world leaders series)
  Bibliography: p. 121.
  1. Galbraith, John Kenneth, 1908-   I. Title.
HB119.G33G35   330'.092'4 [B]   74-14590
ISBN 0-8057-3681-6

TO

EMILE ORPHEUS ALCEDE COSCHINA
My first teacher of economics

Contents

About The Author

John S. Gambs was born in Guatemala where his father and mother (natives of Alsace) were living on a coffee plantation. At age three he left with his parents for the United States, living first in Cleveland and later in Washington, D.C. He graduated from George Washington University and received a Ph.D. in economics at Columbia University. From 1937 to 1940 he was a member of the United States permanent delegation to the International Labor Office in Geneva, Switzerland. Returning to the United States in 1940, he taught at Louisiana State University for two years. During World War II he worked for the War Labor Board.

In 1946 he moved with his wife and two children to Clinton, New York, and taught economics at Hamilton College for twenty-one years, serving as Chairman of the Department of Economics for sixteen. He continues to reside in Clinton as Emeritus Professor of Economics from Hamilton College and enjoys traveling and gardening.

Among his publications are *The Decline of the I.W.W.* (1932), *Beyond Supply and Demand* (1946), *Man, Money and Goods* (1952) and an unorthodox textbook for undergraduates entitled *Economics and Man* (1959). A long-standing interest in the work of John Kenneth Galbraith has prompted him to write this book.

John S. Gambs was one of the founders and early presidents of the Association for Evolutionary Economics and is now Chairman of the Editorial Board of *The Journal of Economic Issues,* the magazine published by this organization.

Preface

This book summarizes and evaluates the work of John Kenneth Galbraith as a social scientist, particularly as a heterodox economist. A heterodox economist, as that phrase will be used in this book, is a professionally trained economist who, having received standard training, usually in one of the accredited universities of the so-called free world, has repudiated many of the basic doctrines held and taught by his trainers. He must know what he is repudiating — as Luther knew what he was doing when he posted his ninety-five theses. I do not here include Marxists as modern heterodox economists, since they have an orthodoxy of their own and follow an Hegelian methodology that is not totally at odds with standard economic methodology. I also exclude liberals. An economist can, without being heterodox, advocate consumerism, abolition of capital punishment, sexual permissiveness, closing of personal income tax loopholes, racial equality, rigorous interpretation of the free-speech and free-press amendments to the Constitution, euthanasia, world peace through the U.N., and so on. The heterodox economist may and often does advocate all or most of the items in the listing above, but to be blown-in-the-glass, he must also repudiate many of the doctrines that standard theory holds dear. It would take a separate book to develop this point fully, but a few things can be said now to suggest what must be wholly or partially repudiated. The heterodox economist must, among other things, disown —

1. the doctrine of marginal productivity as a basis for a theory of distribution;
2. the doctrine of consumer sovereignty;
3. the competitive model, even if amended and modified;
4. the belief that the search for private gain is transmogrified into the public good;
5. the belief that the law of comparative advantage explains much about foreign trade.

The preceding items are a mere sample and are negative rather than positive. The job of describing the differences positively has been done well by others. For those who wish to go further, I strongly recommend Allan G. Gruchy's *Contemporary Economic Thought,* chapter 7.* His description of neoinstitutionalism in that chapter accords with the concept of economic heterodoxy as apprehended in this book.

JOHN S. GAMBS

Acknowledgments

Many people have helped me to get these pages together, and to them I would express my warmest thanks. Jacob Oser of Utica College induced me to write the book and helped me in many ways. My friend Paul Parker was a genial and painstaking editor. A few acquaintances and friends of Galbraith's allowed me to interview them and gave me facts which helped me to complete my picture of the man. They were — in no special order — Harry Erdman, Paul Taylor, Charles Gulick, John Blair, Dorothy Pilkington, E. H. Dwight, Alberta Bigelow, and Seymour Harris.

To Joseph Haden, an old friend, and to my cousin, Jeanne Michel, to K. William Kapp, and Derek C. Jones, I owe thanks for finding and sending me certain publications about Galbraith originating in Europe. The librarians of Hamilton College were most helpful and patient, particularly Helene Browning, Vittoria Mondolfo, and L. Evelyn Canfield. For clerical help beyond the call of duty I am indebted to Carol Cratty and Bonnie Bowie.

An old saying has it that behind every book written by a heterodox economist there stands a woman who, among other things keeps the roofers, plumbers, TV repairmen and assorted bellringers at bay. In this case that woman was my wife, Alice Chase Gambs, and to her I am grateful for this and much else besides.

Chronology

1908   Born October 15 in Iona Station, "Scotch" Canada, the son of William and Catherine Galbraith. Breathed in the Calvanism of the Scotch Canadian colony.

1931   Graduated with a B.S. degree from the Ontario Agricultural College, then a branch of the University of Toronto.

1931- Studied agricultural economics at the University of California in Berkeley.
1933

1933- Taught at an agricultural branch of the University of California and completed requirements for a Ph.D. in economics in 1934.
1934

1934   Taught for a short time at Harvard.

1934- Peripatetic scholar and researcher, in and out of government and academic institutions in the United States and abroad.
1941

1937   Married Catherine Atwater, a student at Radcliffe.

1941- Deputy Administrator of the Office of Price Administration.
1943

1943   Joined the editorial board of *Fortune*.

1949   Returned to Harvard, which has become his home base despite travels and assignments around the world.

1952   Served as speech writer and advisor to Adlai Stevenson during presidential campaign. After Stevenson's defeat, Galbraith served during the Eisenhower administration as chairman of the domestic policy committee of the Democratic Advisory Council. Published *American Capitalism: the Concept of Countervailing Power* which made his name well-known.

1958   Published *The Affluent Society*.

1960   Worked as an active campaigner for John F. Kennedy and upon Kennedy's becoming President was appointed Ambassador to India.

1961-1963 Tour of duty in India.

1963 Returned to Harvard. Continued to work for President Kennedy until Kennedy's death in November.

1967 Published *The New Industrial State*, which has sold more than a million copies.

1968 Worked for Senator Eugene McCarthy and supported his stand against the war in Asia.

1972 Worked for Senator McGovern and debated issues with William F. Buckley, Jr. during the 1972 Democratic convention.

1973 Published *Economics and the Public Purpose*, his most complete book on economics.

CHAPTER 1

Galbraith, The Man

To those who read books and the dollar magazines, John Kenneth Galbraith stands out as a brilliant name. Its owner, six feet eight inches high, is an economist, satirist, litterateur, politician, scholar, publicist, aesthete, diplomat, wit, charmer, reformer, attractive nuisance, and so on, as I shall detail. When he is fearfully and wonderfully arrayed in his ambassadorial top hat, he seems to reach to the sky, and he is perhaps vain enough to believe that this is only just. But his vanity has the saving graces of self-mockery and humor, which make him, like G. B. Shaw, quite bearable to his readers and, no doubt, to those who know him well enough to call him "Ken," for he does not like the name John. He gets more space in the *New York Times Index* than Zsa Zsa Gabor. He just misses the kind of fame that overtook Dorothy Parker and Calvin Coolidge, who were not only widely quoted, but also had characteristic yet unspoken *bons mots* attributed to them. Although only recently established in a dictionary of quotations, his phrases "countervailing power," "affluent society," and "conventional wisdom" are found everywhere. He is widely paraphrased among the literate and even among some of the illiterate. It is safe to say that he will make many more memorable phrases before he makes Paradise — for which he is clearly predestined.

But let's begin at the other end. John Kenneth Galbraith was born in 1908 in "Scotch" Canada on the northern shore of Lake Erie. A straight line from Buffalo to Detroit is about 200 miles long. Very little of that line goes through the United States. It dips into the Canadian waters of Lake Erie, and when it emerges to go overland it lies in the Queen's domain. About halfway on this line sits the town of Dutton, east of which lies Iona Station, where Galbraith says he was born. Neither of these names appears on the maps of an ordinary home atlas.

The Galbraith clan was one of the more highly regarded clans and the father was a "man of standing" — to use the Scotch-Canadian phrase — in that farming community. Very poor and very rich did not exist but social stratification did, and the lowest members of the society were hired men, drunks, lazy farmers, and ignorant ones. The ambient air was highly charged with Calvinism and work for work's sake. Little Ken,[1] who at that age *was* little, went through the local grammar school in five years and then to the community high school. In his autobiographical pages describing those years, published under the title of *The Scotch,* he describes no psychological traumatic events or particularly sad experiences. The high-school principal did indeed seem to be sadistic and ignorant, but the tone of the book is gay and big Ken now describes him amiably as "an old fart."

His college, a modest one, was the Ontario Agricultural College at Guelph, Canada, then a branch of the University of Toronto, from which he was graduated in 1931, at the age of 23. In that year, armed with a B.S. and an offer to become a research assistant at the University of California, this ungilded youth set out for Berkeley. Thus, like Madame de Pompadour — who, it has been told, was a disciple of François Quesnay's — he started out in life as an agricultural economist. I find no description of him at the beginning of this journey. Was this tall, lank, undoubtedly gawky immigrant a little unsure of himself as he set out for the gleaming alabaster cities of the Bay Area? Or was he one of those remarkably self-assured young provincials like the Gascon, D'Artagnan, who, though he arrived in Paris on a raw-boned, yellow nag, with only three small pieces of silver but full of pluck, never faltered and immediately found a place with men who counted and ultimately became a marshal of France? Whatever the answer, the farm boy from Iona Station has become the friend of a president, of presidential candidates, and has met a swarm of heads of states and prime ministers and a vast gaggle of ordinary ministers of state. He has written best sellers — a remarkable achievement for an economist. He has been received by the jet set, the beautiful people, and he knew the Camelot of the Kennedy days. Last, and perhaps least, he was made president of the American Economic Association in 1972.

In 1931, he set out by jalopy for Berkeley to become a research assistant in the department of agricultural economics. On the way, at a crossroads garage in Iowa, he heard a cracker-barrel discussion of Herbert Hoover, then President. The argument, he says, made him a lifelong Democrat — a decision he has little cause to regret. Despite the low station of agricultural economists in the academic hierarchy — a snobbish grading system where abstraction and finical knowledge stand at the top — and despite his depression wage of sixty dollars a month, he enjoyed his new life tremendously. He met interesting fellow students, stimulating teachers, and outside lecturers. After two years of this, punctuated by small increases in salary, he went to the town of Davis near Sacramento, where he taught at an agricultural branch of the university at a yearly salary of $1800. One day he got an offer from Harvard to take an instructorship at $2400. He loved California and wanted to stay, but he rashly used the offer to bargain for a higher salary at California. However, the dean outmaneuvered him, and Galbraith had no choice but to go to Harvard.

He had by now picked up his Ph.D. at Berkeley and had learned a lot about nonagricultural economics. He was thoroughly grounded in neoclassical economics and acknowledges a considerable debt to Alfred Marshall and to Ewald Grether, the California professor who drilled him in the famous *Principles*. He was also influenced by Veblen and Marx; Keynes came later, after the publication of the *General Theory,* obviously.

Much of the above account of his march from Iona Station, via Berkeley, to Cambridge is cribbed from his Berkeley essay in *Economics, Peace and Laughter.* The story is told with a modesty that will surprise some of his readers, who are perhaps fooled by his deviations from bashfulness. To go from student at Ontario Agricultural College to teacher at Harvard University in three years is rather a feat. But he makes it seem like the virtually automatic promotion of most of us from the third to the fourth grade.

He did not stay long at Harvard, however; he became a sort of peripatetic scholar, teacher, investigator, and researcher, in and out of government and academic institutions, here and abroad. In 1941 at the age of thirty-three he came to rest temporarily in Washington, when he became deputy administrator of the Office of Price Administration — a job that made him virtually the economic czar of the United States until he left in 1943. In his *Theory of Price Control* we get a moderately full account of his work as a price controller. It is interesting to note in passing that this man, who has had as much price-control experience as anybody in the free world, was not consulted when, in 1971, Nixon instituted price, wage, and other controls.

In the spring of 1945 he became one of the directors of the United States Strategic Bombing Survey. Among his colleagues were

George Ball and Paul Nitze. Apparently Franklin Roosevelt, in 1944, had begun to wonder whether the American air force had really done as much to hamper Germany's war production as it thought it had. The postwar survey, conducted by those spoken of above, along with a team of American and British economists and statisticians found — to be brief — that the air force had vastly overrated its capacity to obstruct German war production. The findings annoyed the air force, Galbraith observes. And he has since, if sometimes only casually, expressed doubt as to how much military damage flying machines could do, or did, in Korea and Indochina.

Galbraith married at the age of twenty-nine. His wife, Catherine Atwater, was sixteen inches shorter than he and studying at Radcliffe after her graduation from Smith College. They have had four sons; the first died young. Although no economist, perhaps, has published as many autobiographical words as Galbraith, he has many reticences and maintains a certain privacy. Yet one does gather that family life is very happy for the Galbraiths. She has, incidentally, written charmingly about being an ambassador's wife and, more recently about India, with Rama Mehta. Galbraith and his sons John and James took part in the 1972 Democratic convention and, on the eve of its opening, all three appeared on a television program. Father and sons made a good impression on viewers in my circle of friends. Between January and July of 1972, Galbraith had grown lots of hair and had almost caught up with his sons.

In 1943 he joined the editorial board of *Fortune.* He wanted editorial and writing experience and, by his own account, Henry Luce helped him a good deal. After *Fortune,* he went back to Harvard in 1949. Harvard has been his base ever since.

We turn now to a brief summary of Galbraith's political career. I have already written that on his jalopy trip from Iona Station to Berkeley, while still a Canadian citizen, he decided to become a lifelong Democrat.

At Harvard, as a teacher, Galbraith had come in contact with the young Kennedys, first with Joseph Kennedy, Jr., killed in the Second World War, then with John F. Kennedy, both of them students. These meetings may have helped to move Galbraith nearer to the center of the Democratic party, though he was by no means an obscure bureaucrat in the early 1940's of Franklin Roosevelt. In any event, in 1952, we find him in the entourage of Adlai Stevenson during the Presidential campaign of that year, advising and writing speeches for Adlai.

During the Eisenhower administration, following Stevenson's defeat, he was chairman of the domestic policy committee of the Democratic Advisory Council. His relation to the party, he has written, during his thirty-odd years of activity within it, have ranged from uneasy to unpleasant.[2] When John F. Kennedy became a possible presidential candidate, Galbraith began to work for him, to the discomfiture of some of his liberal associates. By now he had become widely known as a liberal through his books and otherwise, and his choice of John Kennedy was not applauded by some of his friends, including Eleanor Roosevelt. At that time I still had contact with former New Deal colleagues (I had held a few minor federal jobs in the 1930's), and they felt lukewarm about Kennedy for several reasons. One reason was his silence on Senator Joseph McCarthy; another was the fear that he might oppose attempts to legalize birth control and abortion, even though it was known that these are matters for state action.

After the nomination Galbraith worked actively for his candidate not only as an advisor — the phrase "brains trust" was now out of fashion — but also as an active campaigner. Kennedy won and Galbraith was now inside a most exalted circle.

In his *Ambassador's Journal,* subtitled *A Personal Account of the Kennedy Years,* he has much of interest to say about the jobs he did between the election and the Kennedy inauguration, or, more precisely, before he left for his Indian mission. About a month after the election Kennedy asked Galbraith if he would like to be ambassador to India. The answer was yes, with pleasure, but would he be more useful as senator from Massachusetts? The president replied that, "five to one," he would be more useful in New Delhi, and that settled that. The month before inauguration was a busy one for Galbraith. He wrote speeches for Kennedy, or, at least, drafted sections of speeches, acted as talent scout for junior and senior cabinet posts, and met with fellow economists to suggest various policies, among them policies relating to the problem of gold outflow (I mention this particularly because — until very recently — he had not elsewhere written on international trade). He made several contributions to the Inaugural Address, his favorite and least amended ones being, apparently, that we should give foreign aid "not to defeat communism, not to win votes, but because it is right," and that "we should never negotiate out of fear, but never fear to negotiate."

Until April, 1961, when Galbraith left for India, he worked on a wide range of economic problems relating to the new administration's policies and on the messages that flow from the White House to the Capitol between Twelfth Night and Ash Wednesday. On April 9, 1961, he arrived in New Delhi. Many persons who, like myself, had read his economic writings and had desultorily followed his political activities wondered whether he had, in effect, been gently exiled by the new President. Might it not be a handicap to have such an articulate liberal so visibly near the center of power? Whatever the answer, it must be observed that Galbraith was not completely forgotten in his distant post. The fast jets were now widely available. He came back to Washington often enough for Republicans to comment not that he "was neglecting India but that he was insufficiently neglecting the United States."[3] He wrote long letters directly to Kennedy on both foreign and domestic issues. After visiting Indochina, he suggested keeping out of there. The embassy itself was invaded by a fantastically large crowd of American officials and legislators on business and on junkets. Mrs. Kennedy's (Jackie's) visit to India did not help to keep her host's name and pictures off the front pages at home. Once, when the first lady had spent rather a lot on a shopping tour, presumably under Galbraith's guidance, she explained her seeming extravagance to reporters by telling them that, since Ken was an economist, he didn't know much about prices — or, at least, that is what one newspaper printed.

The tour of duty in India was not easy. There was plenty of chaos in Asia and Foggy Bottom to keep the ambassador busy. Krishna Menon and Dean Rusk were crosses to bear. The interrelations of China, India, and Pakistan demanded knowledge, wisdom, and judgment. The food and climate were not always bearable. He was often very weary and his sinuses bothered him. He complains of insomnia in his *Journal* and confesses to considerable reliance on sleeping pills — which he seems to prefer to liquor, for some reason. But it is clear that he enjoyed his work. In addition he wrote large parts of at least two books during this period.

He had been granted a two-years' leave of absence from Harvard, and, although this might have been extended, he decided to come home. This he did in July, 1963. In August, he handled a dispute over airline rights between the United States and Canada. The Canadian prime minister selected Galbraith to represent Canadian interests and Kennedy selected Galbraith to represent American interests. The dispute was quickly settled to everybody's satisfaction.

On November 22, Kennedy was assassinated. Galbraith helped

with funeral arrangements and stayed around briefly to give
assistance to the new President. He ends his *Journal* by writing:

> Then I had lunch with Arthur [Schlesinger, Jr.] who was much more com-
> posed and, I think, partly reconciled to the thought of coming back to Cam-
> bridge. But not completely reconciled. Then we caught the two-thirty plane
> home.

Since then Galbraith's political life has been much less active,
though by no means quiescent. He and President Johnson were not
hostile, but obviously the new president had his own friends. The
enlargement of the war in Vietnam would perhaps have caused friction between the two men had they long been thrown together. In the
1968 campaign Galbraith, presumably attracted by Senator Eugene
McCarthy's stand against the worsening Asian conflict, worked for
him as a presidential candidate. In a letter to me he wrote: "The person I campaigned for most diligently, which means raising money,
was Eugene McCarthy." He wrote against the war, against the large
role of the Pentagon in American life, and urged wage and price controls. He felt that the Democratic party needed reform and has not
hesitated to tell his party how to reform itself.

In a *Playboy* interview[4] Galbraith rather movingly and eloquently
states that he has never so deeply and exclusively devoted himself to
any cause as he has to the termination of the war in Vietnam. He
speaks of having helped to organize, to write ads, and of having given
aid to members of Congress who opposed the fighting. Reading this I
was reminded of the Philosophical Radicals who, in similar fashion,
worked to achieve so many reforms in England a century and a half
ago.

In the 1972 campaign, he worked for Senator McGovern. Many
watched him with William F. Buckley on the Today Show during the
1972 Democratic Convention. Some have said that for this he should
not easily be forgiven. Incidentally, I once asked him whether he was
really a friend of Buckley. His reply was that Buckley was one of the
most intelligent conservatives in America and that his wit was
worthy of admiration. The two men are neighbors in Gstaad,
Switzerland. As he spoke, it flashed through my mind that I had once
met an Israeli and an Arab on the American college lecture circuit
who debated hotly almost every night before their young audiences
but traveled fraternally together and ate breakfast at the same table

at the same time in the coffee shoppes of their hotels. I am told that professional wrestlers have similar amiable relationships. Clarence E. Ayres and Frank Knight, economists of vastly differing views, are also said to have had warm personal regard for one another. Well, as is widely known, Galbraith's entry lost again: Stevenson twice, McCarthy once, and then McGovern. The Watergate incident is well developed as I write. Like many Democrats, Galbraith has been silent. Indeed, the only thing I have found by him on current events has been an article in the *New York Times* on four species of the genus publicist, which has nothing to do with the Watergate incident.

Galbraith will probably never seek elected office, though predictions of this sort are rash. Men do not normally pursue office for the first time when they are within hailing distance of Medicare, unless it be some lowly, local post like dog warden. He has in the past thought about a governorship, or senate seat, but he has, apparently, given up such ideas. In the *Playboy* interview he spoke earnestly of the great pleasures of authorship, and if he has any regrets about the course of his life they revolve around his coming so late to writing. Writing gives him a sense of liberation which is very sweet to him, he says, and he wishes he had begun sooner. But all this does not really mean that he will stay out of politics. He is, even now, being consulted by high-ranking Democrats and if a congenial member of his party should be elected in 1976, it is hard to see how he could stay out of the kitchen cabinet, at least. One suspects that he would not be asked to fill a regular cabinet job, and, anyhow, he himself would probably not like to be tied down to a desk job in Washington. But what fun it would be to see him running the Department of State.

We may, then, expect from him primarily new books and pamphlets on the current economic and political scene, and on sociology and economic history. His range is wide and he does not limit himself to the issue that intrigues the little thinkers of the dismal science, namely, the disposal of scarce goods.

Since much of the remainder of the book will be devoted to Galbraith the writer, primarily of economics, this is as appropriate a place as any to try to picture Galbraith as a total personality. He is complex. Franz Kafka has said that one never understands the living, and I must confess that this truth has been a major difficulty in confecting this book. All writers reveal themselves to their readers for, *le style est l'homme même;* and to go beyond Buffon's phrase, no *style,* no *homme,* which is perhaps why so many articles in the social-science quarterlies make such dull reading. With Galbraith there is plenty of *style* and plenty of *homme;* hence, there is plenty of self-revelation, but not quite enough. He also tells us much through his autobiographical articles and books. But still he eludes us. At the age of thirty-three he was already an important bureaucrat, and one feels that he learned early through press conferences and otherwise not only to tell much but also to conceal much. When it began to leak out that Mark Epernay, the author of a satirical book, was really Galbraith, then ambassador to India, *Newsweek* cabled, "Are you Mark Epernay? Please confirm or deny." Galbraith cabled back "Who is Mark Epernay?" Skill of this sort presents problems for Galbraith watchers. In *The Scotch,* the book concerned with his childhood, he is not introspective; he does not tell us what he dreamed of as a child or stripling, his back on fresh meadow grass, looking at the sky. Did he shout snatches of romantic poetry as he walked alone in a grove? He does speak of girl friends — or, at least, of one captivating maiden — but did he ever dwell deliciously on the thought that she would weep at his grave if he should kill himself or waste away from an obscure disease? No, it was all good fun up there at Iona Station — no sorrows of a young Werther, no brooding melancholy such as a Lamartine felt upon revisiting his *Lac.*

He does make clear in *The Scotch* that he breathed deeply of the ambient Calvinistic air. The influence of this is still with him. None of Calvin's followers ever worked much harder than he. He writes on planes and composes paragraphs in his head when he listens to bores even in conversations *à deux.* He improves each shining hour, as the excellent hymnist observed about the little busy bee. His tone is unfailingly moral and his indignation, when aroused, is righteous and like a sledgehammer. But his morality is that of a stern social ethicist not that of the bluenose. Often the humor of a sentence arises out of ironical use of a phrase that originated in a prayerbook or the Scriptures.

He is something of a showman. The cover of one of his books describes him as the American master of the put-on. Jack Benny, in his more active years, created an image of himself as a close-fisted, perpetually thirty-nine, gifted violinist. In somewhat the same fashion, Galbraith has contributed to the image of a man with small modesty. He has exhibited rather more than a grain of arrogance. The arrogance, however, is often scaled down to impudence or mischievousness. Though he can be ingratiating, I have been told by those who have seen much more of him than I that he is not always so. He has said, when evaluating his own work highly, that he never allows modesty to stand in the way of truth. If he thinks he has been hit under the belt — say in a review of one of his books — he will, like Winston Churchill, mobilize the English language to strike back — strike back rather than defend himself.

He confesses to being a liberal Democrat and a reformer; yet he often speaks of liberals in the third person, as if to distinguish himself from the lesser breeds. This comes about, I think, because liberals tend to have their own conventional wisdom, and one of his efforts is to get away from all conventional wisdom, at least in the social sciences. Both right and left now entertain — whatever may have been true of the past — outmoded notions, or models, of our society and of our economic system.

Coming now to very minor points. He does not smoke and his drinking is moderate. He likes parties within reason. Perhaps it is an inverse Calvinism that makes him introduce a few racy stories in his writing. He likes to ski but concedes that he does not ski as well as Jean-Claude Killy. He swims, skates, and hikes. He divides most of his time left over from Cambridge and Washington between a place in Vermont and a chalet in Gstaad.

The question of his income comes up from time to time in *ad hominem* fashion. It is sometimes said he is too rich to be really sincere about economic reform, and a few college students of the left seem to feel that so much (apparent) money must qualify him only for membership in the establishment. The latter half of his life has undoubtedly been comfortable, and he has no doubt been able to make his martinis with "Beefeater" rather than "Oriskany Valley Belle," but he was not born with a silver spoon in his mouth. However, this whole business is taradiddle. His income is none of our affair. The poor have had friends born wealthy from Buddha to Roosevelt, and enemies from ribbon clerks to itinerant coster-mongers.

His physical appearance is impressive and pleasing. He is tall, slender and well-proportioned, like some of the better-built basket-ball players — not at all stork-like and not a hint of entasis. On the dustjackets of two of his books, there are interesting camera studies of him. One shows him full-length, deep in the ferns of a coppice. He wears slacks and a bush coat. His weight rests mainly on his right foot; the left comes forward and shares the residual burden with a rustic cane. His thick hair is unobtrusively parted and one shock of it cascades down to his right eye. The general effect is that of a nature lover, sort of unposed, but not entirely. The second photo includes only the head and shoulders, the latter very dark. Shirt, coat, and tie are also nearly black. This picture is dramatic and clearly posed. I showed it to some friends who had never met him and knew him only through television and the printed word. Their comments were: strong, intelligent, egocentric, no misgivings about his abilities, courageous, witty, charming, face of a successful actor like Richard Burton, calculating, cautious, shrewd, skeptical, watchful, ironic, observant, intense, brooding, searching, serious. One woman said, "My sympathies go with Kitty" (his wife); another commented concerning his nose, "I see why the cartoonists make him look like a toucan." I think he himself, when dwelling on his virtues, likes to think of himself as lacking in solemnity and piety; but none of the latter-day Lavaters among my friends spotted this. Neither did they note what a long-term friend and associate of Galbraith's told me about him: that he was a man of great honesty and courage.

Whatever the physiognomists have to say about him, it is clear that we are considering a greatly talented, paradoxical, and complex person, gifted in several fields. He is perhaps one of the most interesting men alive.

CHAPTER 2

Forces That Molded
Galbraith's Thinking

I asked Galbraith in a letter what economists other than
Keynes had influenced him. I left out Keynes because
Galbraith's writings adequately describe the considerable effect the
Englishman has had on him. His reply was: " . . . I was most influenced by Marshall, Veblen and, of course, Marx. I would have
great difficulty placing them in order." Thus we have, without going
to much trouble, a fairly concise answer to the central question of
this chapter: What forces have molded Galbraith's thought? And yet
the answer is not wholly satisfying. Why did they influence him, especially Marx and Veblen?[1]

Marshall and Keynes are easy enough to explain. Training in
Marshall was as basic to the curriculum of the graduate school of
economics in the period 1930 - 33 as toilet training is to the
curriculum of the nursery school today. Keynes, a little later, was as
visible as a vast shower of shooting stars. Nobody in economics could
ignore him, and though it was a bit dashing to embrace him in the
thirties, and though a dreadful war intervened to slow down scholarly
pursuits, American economists had to be well schooled in
Keynesianism before the 1950's, and most of them accepted him. But
to do more than nod coldly in the direction of Veblen and Marx required positive effort, and the effort, when made, was unrewarded. A
Galbraith watcher wonders how he was dragged down into this
"underworld of economics," to use one of Keynes's condescending
phrases. William James has suggested that the world is divided into
the tough-minded and the tender-minded. Marx and Veblen were
tough-minded and the perhaps the same may be said of Galbraith. It
may have been a question of genes or of Galbraith's solution of the
Oedipus problem or the result of a traumatic love affair — all of
them inviting speculation that is out of bounds here.

If one reviews his life, environmental explanations do flock to mind, though their reliability is open to question. In the autobiography of his early years *(The Scotch)* one sees dimly the possible sources of heresy. In the first decade of this century the land around Lake St. Clair and Georgian Bay did not harbor gun-toting gamblers or horse thieves, but something of the frontier spirit probably clung to the isolated farming villages. There was respect for hard, manual work and a pragmatic temper prevailed. As at all frontiers, if Clarence E. Ayres is to be believed, the hold of tradition is weaker in the new communities than in the old. One wonders how much — or whether — this had to do with the informing of his attitudes. Neither his father nor his mother is described as a dissenter, although his father, a British subject, is reported to have said that kings ought to be compelled to take examinations before being crowned. Canadians — or, at least the Scotch Canadians — were not fired by imperial patriotism to fight against the Kaiser. The welkin above Iona Station presumably rang but feebly to the strains of *Tipperary* or *Madelon.* Perhaps the tepid patriotism of these Canadians revealed to young Galbraith that one could be decent and upright, yet abstain from flecking the Argonne with patriotic gore.

In Galbraith's introduction to an edition of Veblen's *Theory of the Leisure Class* he likens the Scandinavian farming communities of the Midwest that harbored the Veblens to the Scotch farming community of Ontario that sheltered the Galbraith clan. The cultivators of both areas felt a yeomanly sense of worth based on frugality, capacity for hard work. And they often had more money in the bank than the city folks. But the people in the towns, even if lowly poolroom operators, felt that social prestige lay with them. They professed the more fashionable religions; they identified themselves, however fatuously, with the ruling classes. They regarded the farmers as country bumpkins. Veblen and Galbraith resented the self-appointed elite and, in later life, both men revenged the slights of their youth through their writing.

In his early twenties, in Berkeley, there is more tangible information about the sources of growing dissent. The faculty harbored a few dissenters. He lived there during some of the worst years of the depression. He was lucky enough and able enough to get a modest job, but he was aware of the fact that some of his gifted classmates were jobless. Although Galbraith left California before the Oakies arrived, he could scarcely have been unaware of the social turmoil there. Upton Sinclair was about to run for governor. The problem of migratory labor and the memory of the desperate I.W.W. were disturbing. A so-called barter movement was springing up — really a rebellious movement to form producers' cooperatives — everywhere, but especially in California and Utah. The Townsend Plan was developed in California. It was simple, the mechanics ingeniously geared to prevent hoarding, and it won enough publicity to come to the attention of all, including economists. About the same time, in Galbraith's native Canada, the social credit plan and the Cooperative Commonwealth Federation were being discussed and partially implemented.

His life in California was dominated by down-to-earth research, such as the study of the prices of figs and prunes. This involved the most exoteric and matter-of-fact methodology, which must have collided with the esoteric concepts of standard theory: equilibrium, value, pure competition, marginal productivity, and other Cartesian inheritances.

Concurrently came Roosevelt, the New Deal, and Keynes. Standard theory was turned inside out by events. The equilibrium of full employment was not being reestablished by natural law or automatic forces or anything else and to a young economist with an open and inquiring mind, it must have been stirring that a man of Keynes's stature was saying that full employment was the the special case not the general case. Though Keynesian economics does not receive top grades from modern dissenters, it was widely acclaimed as a breakthrough in its day. Anybody could see that it was a damaging lunge at the nonsensical orthodox depression theory of the past. It was easy for any early convert to Keynes to see that other heterodox economists like Veblen and Marx were not wholly wrong.

So much for an attempt to explain why he was attracted to Veblen and Marx. I gather that, in chronological order, Galbraith was exposed first to Marshall, second to Veblen and Marx, and last to Keynes. This does not mean that each stage supplanted the preceding stage. By the time Galbraith began writing in earnest he had already been exposed to the economists who have influenced him most strongly and his writings may be considered a blend of all four plus, of course, whatever originality was his, and the work of scores of run-of-the-mill scholars we all read.

What have Veblen and Marx contributed to Galbraith? We consider them together not because Veblen is a latter-day Marxist but because they have well-known similarities, despite Veblen's clear repudiation of Marx and of his Hegelianism. Some devout Veblenians would say that Galbraith owes everything to Veblen, but this is going a little too far. In any case, as we examine his work more closely in later chapters, we shall take note of certain specific Veblenian influences. But I must mention here two of Veblen's theories that did not influence him. A cardinal theory of Veblen's is the sharp distinction he makes between pecuniary and industrial employment — the former allied to the constructive propensities of mankind, the latter to the aggressive propensities. This theme is not woven into Galbraith's fabric. The second is Veblen's theory of social change, which revolves around the tensions between money-makers and goods-makers — a tension that may result in conflict of uncertain outcome. The nearest Galbraith comes to this is his suggestion that the educational and scientific estate may help to improve the quality of life — something to be discussed later.

Almost every reviewer of his books comments on the similarities between Veblen and Galbraith: irony, playfulness, understatement, satire, humor, wit, and so forth. How much is imitation and how much the inevitable product of seeing orthodox economics and scholarship in general with a jaundiced eye? It would be unclever to say that if you have read one social critic you've read them all, but Anatole France, G. B. Shaw, Voltaire, Swift, Orwell — to name a few — have a family resemblance and Galbraith belongs in the family. Nonetheless there are differences in style between Veblen and Galbraith.

The latter uses self-mockery rather charmingly to make more palatable what I shall have to call egotism. Veblen conceals his egotism by lofty scholarship, sesquipedalianism, and a self-effacing, almost mousey, style. He rarely or never uses the first person singular; Galbraith is very free with his *I's*. Veblen demands more from his readers; Galbraith obviously tries for the pellucid, but misses it sometimes. Galbraith rather enjoys ribbing many of his acquaintances, which include the great of the world, especially the great in politics. Poor Veblen rarely met great men, except other scholars: Jacques Loeb, John Dewey, Albert Michelson. Galbraith's style when he is provoked goes as far as pugnaciousness, Veblen's rather often to sadism. Galbraith coddles and conciliates his readers. In the foreword to his *American Capitalism,* for example, he says that "this is a good-humored book," even though it "is an essay in social criticism." Veblen never tries to placate. Veblen was an eccentric scholar; Galbraith is a smoothie and a man of the world. The older man would have liked to live in a different kind of society, but his style reflects little of the reformer's zeal; indeed, taken on the

whole, one could almost characterize it as *le je-m'en-foutisme*.
Veblen used the vocabulary of the more exact sciences even in his
humor; he is probably the only writer who can make you laugh at the
use of the word "monocotyledonous." Galbraith rather avoids the
vocabulary of science, but he exhorts, often with fervor; he is after all
a Democrat and a reformer.   Veblen is roundabout, Galbraith is
direct. Even so, reading him steadily for a fortnight or so is a little
like having too much champagne and caviar. One yearns for an
honest beer and some upper New York State cheese with water
biscuits. If Galbraith's and Veblen's ideas had been set forth in
plainer English, with the juvenile humor and odious prose of the
average economist, it is doubtful whether either would have attracted
much attention; " 'tis his at last who says it best."

From both Veblen and Marx, Galbraith gets the sense of institutional change. It would perhaps be more nearly exact to say that,
like Veblen and Marx, Galbraith *has* a sense of institutional change.
He may have acquired this as a little boy at Iona Station, but to
make things easier for both reader and author, we shall here and
elsewhere say that he was influenced by Marx and Veblen — since
they were his seniors — rather than that he picked up things in-
dependently and then found, to everybody's surprise, that they con-
formed to Veblenism and Marxism. Standard theory, with the excep-
tion of a few practitioners, has little sense of institutional change. Its
roots lie in the subscience of mechanics, which has no need for an
evolutionary outlook; it is a two-dimensional, billiard-ball science.
To be sure, it does see quantitative change: growth of the GNP, of
population, of the size of firms, decline of farming. But such changes
are not seen as causes or partial causes of basic institutional change,
or as demanding basic institutional change if man is to get more than
peripheral benefits or harm from them. Veblen and Marx saw an
evolution[2] of social institutions and Galbraith sees this too. The
changes he speaks of are qualitative. This matter will be further
analyzed as we discuss individual works in succeding chapters.

Like Veblen and Marx, Galbraith is a kind of determinist.
However, I do not think that Marx and Galbraith are true determinists, whereas Veblen is. Determinism applied to human affairs is
usually opposed to the concept of free will. This duality is
theologically useful. If one's will is free, one can be held responsible
for good deeds as well as for sins, and one can go to heaven or hell
depending on the choices made between good and evil. But in scientific discourse free will has no place. In the social sciences we may

speak of geographic determinism or economic determinism and other kinds as well. Thus, we can say that the inhabitants of coastal areas will eat more fish and other fruits of the sea than inland dwellers. Or we can say that exalted events, such as the Crusades, were caused by economic forces. Or we can say, on a different level, that certain forces already set in motion are bound to work themselves out. Thus, we can predict that color television will improve and that its cost, in constant dollars, will go down. What is important in this last example is that television sets will improve without exhortation, educational campaigns, evangelism, legislation, or proselytizing effort.

In psychology, determinism means that there is a cause for all human behavior. Freud is a determinist. Slips of the tongue, as is well-known, may be a sort of compromise between what is socially acceptable and what is not. They are not random accidents. Freud — or was it Brill? — tells about the courtly senior citizen who, listening politely to a young woman's piano playing and under the influence of a diuretic, tried to tell her when at length she had struck the last note, that "that was indeed a very difficult piece to play." But his need was so pressing that he transposed a few letters and blurted out his real thoughts. One cannot profess the scientific spirit without being some sort of determinist, else one would have to assert the supremacy of gremlins, incantation, and magic. The real argument among men of scientific bent is not whether determinism is true doctrine, but what determines what.

Marxists are determinists insofar as their doctrines hold that capitalists will, without exhortation, do what they must do, namely, exploit labor, maximize profits, cause unemployment and depressions, precipitate wars, and bring about enough disorder to usher in an Utopian state. This does not mean that their deterministic theories are correct. Indeed, they are not determinists insofar as they seek converts, organize political parties, and actively promote disorder and confusion. All such carryings on would be unnecessary if the contradictions of capitalism would suffice to cause the labefaction of its institutions.

Veblen never wavered in his determinism. Nothing much would ever happen that was not already in the works. It is true that he thought he saw possibilities in a Soviet of technicians or engineers, but he ended by writing that engineers showed no present promise of reforming the economy. He had no faith in new laws, appeals to reason, kindness, courtesy, neighbor-loving, religious impulses, or pity; he did not think that people conditioned by this society could do much to change it. But he did think that the society itself, changed by technology, might bring about changes in human beings, and these changed human beings might bring about beneficent social change. The exogenous cause, technological progress, seems to arise out of a basic human trait: "idle curiosity." He expresses his dogged determinism in one of his most sublime statements:

But history records more frequent and more spectacular instances of the triumph of imbecile institutions over life and culture than of peoples who have by force of instinctive insight saved themselves alive out of a desperately precarious institutional situation, such, for instance, as now faces the peoples of Christendom.[3]

Galbraith, though often classed as a technological determinist, is not like Veblen in this sphere. He is a registered Democrat, active in his party's campaigns, and an unabashed reformer. He even composes hortatory decalogues telling us exactly what to do to achieve certain politico-economic reforms. Exhortation is not a determinist's weapon. Indeed, the dyed-in-the-wool determinist has no weapon at all. Social outcomes, good or bad, will take place without direct and conscious human intervention. Moreover, they may take place as a result of events that had no initial relevance to the outcomes. We may take the case of the automobile, which helped mightily to expand sexual freedom. One may reasonably assume that such automotive pioneers as Karl Benz and Gottlieb Daimler, in 1895, had no idea that they were promoting the sexual revolution that began — let us say — around the 1920's when for the first time in history males and females could drive away from observation and into the wildwood in twenty minutes.

We must, however, note that many reforms Galbraith advocates are within the realm of the feasible in the sense that we are already moving toward some of his goals. He opposes vehemently the seniority system in Congress, and I suppose that this will be changed in the calculable future. He advocated a wage-and-price freeze, and this came in 1971, perhaps faster than he would have predicted. But this, too, was already in the works. Broad medical insurance is in the works. Galbraith seems, instinctively, to recognize gradients down which it is relatively easy to push the cart of social change. Other things appear to him to be lost causes. One of them seems to be the consumers' movement. In 1969 he wrote: "Robert Brady who was the friend of the consumer and other lost causes."[4] Another lost cause is antitrust. Here we have a clear record of eighty-five years of failure — or, more precisely, of mingy effort, for one cannot fail in what one has not tried to do. Galbraith not only has given up trust busting as a lost cause but also feels it might do harm to our way of life now that we are in fact addicted to gigantism.

The New Industrial State gives Galbraith the reputation of being a technological determinist because he appears to believe that the way we produce determines not only the organization of the economy but also many of our beliefs and values. So profound is this influence that he sees convergences between the United States and the Soviet Union as our technological systems come to resemble one another. An interesting observation he makes in this connection is that revolutionary American youth is withdrawing its admiration from the Soviet Union and bestowing it on Cuba and China. But Cuba and China, as they make technological progress, will resemble the United States and Russia. And then the revolutionaries will have to seek their Utopias elsewhere.

I should like to conclude this section by saying that Galbraith, though a wavering determinist, is not an evangelical economist, in spite of his decalogues. He doubts very much that men will hearken to the pleas made by the economic evangelists. Men simply do not like to compete openly and fairly and will always seek a sheltered market, although they will not always succeed, to be sure. They will try to use their political influence — when they have it — not only to get a government contract but also to get an overgenerous and out-rageous one. They will strive for tariff protection, for the right to preempt patents that arise from publicly supported research. And they will often succeed in getting these and other favors. Seeing all this, the standard economist, often politically illiterate and utterly naive besides, suggests that such legislated blocks to competition and countless others be legislated against and that competition be restored. This means that those who granted the favors for self-serving reasons should now undergo a sudden change of heart and nullify the gifts. This is evangelism and makes sense only to fellow evangelists.

Though Galbraith is not always consistent, expecially when he speaks of political reform,[5] he is aware of the impotence of evangelism and avoids more than most men empty exhortation. Because he does not call for the fractionizing of General Motors and other large companies, some of his colleagues accuse him of hating competition and loving the gargantuan corporations. It is doubtful whether any reader of Galbraith's knows what kind of economic firm Galbraith prefers. We know what the fruits of his economic system should be (less noise, dirt, pollution; more beauty and devotion to function, etc.) but we don't know what kinds of firms will achieve these ends.

If Galbraith is not a determinist in the Marx-Veblen sense, he at least avoids urging economic reform by the interaction of Yin and Yang, by incantation and appeals to man's love of fair play and gentlemanly competition. Man responds but feebly to these appeals, if at all. Galbraith seeks to push forward beneficent programs already in motion.

The determinism spoken of above is related to psychology. A determinist would say that free will has little to do with human behavior and that the culture, strongly influenced by technology if not omnipotent in determining behavior, will usually win the day. Galbraith would find in the determinists' argument strong support for his thesis that the technostructure can force the consumer to accept its goods and services; the individual is all but powerless. But we must return to psychology, pure and simple.

Standard economic theorists have little patience with psychology. They concede that economics is a behavioral science but do not allow that knowledge to bother them too much. One of them has even asked whether, when some psychologist comes up with some new idea, the time-tested theories of economics must be rewritten. Of course the onward march of scientific discovery often invalidates previous discovery and often affects sciences other than those in which the new discovery is made. Louis Pasteur was a chemist, but his discoveries altered fundamentally the science and art of medicine. Economics should not be protected from the uncomfortable discoveries made in psychology or any of the other sciences: who do economists think they are, anyhow? But even standard economists must make some assumptions about man, and they do — that is, they invent the psychology they need as they go along. They assume that wants are limitless, that man chooses the greatest profit or the least loss, that he rationally weighs the benefit (pleasure, satisfaction, utility) he gets from any contemplated expenditure against the benefit he might get from some other expenditure. There may be exceptions to all this, they concede, but the less said about them, the better.

No such simple do-it-yourself psychological principles can be disengaged from Veblen and Galbraith, though perhaps Marx comes close to classical and neoclassical thought. Marx does, however, develop one psychological principle of his own, namely, the theory of increasing misery, which, he holds, leads on to revolution. This is probably a false theory since it is more likely that rising expectations, if disappointed, lead to violent action; increasing misery probably leads to despair and inaction. In any case, increasing misery is not part of the Galbraithian scheme. Neither Galbraith nor Veblen has a high regard for human rationality. For both, the underlying population is easily deceived, credulous, subject to mass hysteria, victimized by vanity and pride. We are still dominated by sympathetic magic, myth, envy, resistance to reasonable argument, superstition. Galbraith, in one of his playfully serious moments, has in phantasy invented a phonographic amulet for businessmen to wear. Businessmen's confidence is sustained by this device, which plays the recorded voices of presidents who were in control during hard times, but confidence is weakened by the voices of those who seek to restore good times. One point of this tomfoolery is that businessmen always feel better when they hear from a Hoover such words as liberty, individualism, free enterprise, even when the state of the economy is bad, but are gripped by cold fear when a Roosevelt intervenes to save capitalism. Another point is that men are irrational. As in his observations on social nostalgia he here comments again on the fact that the old incantations are best and do least to disturb complacency. Imaginative action to solve an economic problem is, on the other hand, most disturbing. It is clear, both here and elsewhere, that Galbraith goes beyond the psychology of marketplace rationality, which is what fascinates standard theory, and goes on to the psychology of reform and change.

The Great Crash, 1929 is a book about the madness of speculation, the stupidity of politicians, economists, and other pundits, mass credulity, unwarranted oracularity. The crash betrays the strong desire of man to get something for nothing. It is interesting that no other economist has studied 1929; perhaps it is because orthodox economists believe that men earn or should earn their incomes by the marginal productivity of the sweat in their faces, not by speculation. In *Economics and the Art of Controversy* he ruminates over the senseless debates that persist over issues already settled such as labor's right to organize. Mankind comes off rather badly in *The McLandress Dimension:* egotistical, hypocritical, snobbish, pompous. Veblen sees the same traits. I would not wish to say that Galbraith is more cynical than Veblen, but Veblen does discuss the instincts of workmanship, parental bent, and idle curiosity as forming a complex of constructive instincts;[6] these matters Galbraith ignores.

In summary, one may venture the generalization that Galbraith's psychology is oriented to economic reform: why is man opposed to economic reform; why is man opposed to beneficent change, or, more precisely, why is man so mulish about making changes? Why such inertia? Unlike standard theorists he is interested in diverting man from huckstering his way through eternity.

Standard theory, though anciently known as pessimistic and dismal, has nevertheless been marked by a certain optimism. Poverty was never a fault of human arrangements but rather of the law of diminishing returns, or of the niggardliness of nature, or of the impossibility of jacking up marginal value productivity (as in farming). Men were, of course, greedy; but that was fine because greed transmogrifies itself through the marketplace into a public benefit. In a rocking-horse couplet, Alexander Pope made this clear even before *The Wealth of Nations* appeared: "Thus God and Nature formed the general frame, / And bade self-love and social be the same."

In short, standard theory has always seen a harmony of human interests in economic affairs. There is even a certain delicacy about discussing international warfare and the military-industrial complex in economic textbooks. I say *even* because, while one may understand that internal tensions are unpleasant to talk about before innocent twenty-year-olds, one might at least talk about external conflicts or threats of conflict. But the textbooks present a dulcified world that has existed only in the imagination.

Both Marx and Veblen saw tensions — domestic and foreign — rather than harmony of interest. In Marx, as is known by nearly all, the tension takes the form of the class struggle. In Veblen, the tension lies between the practioners of industrial and pecuniary pursuits, or, more broadly, between those dominated by the constructive propensities and those dominated by the destructive propensities.[7] Galbraith sees tensions of a similar sort in our society; the tension between the technostructure and the educational and scientific estate — a matter to be discussed more fully in a later chapter.

Veblen, Marx, and others are exponents of what might be named "holism" in economics, a word favored by Allan G. Gruchy.[8] I quote him:

The term "holistic" has been selected because it calls attention to what is most characteristic of the new economics: its interest in studying the economic system as an evolving unified whole or synthesis, in the light of which the system's parts take on their full meaning.

This definition is a little abstract but perhaps it can be made more concrete without going back to the Deluge. An economist holding such a concept thinks of the economic system as being a reflection of the entire culture, not as an isolated mechanism that could be introduced in any society. It has a past, present, and future related to the culture in which it is found. As a result economics must draw on history and the other social sciences to explain what is going on in the economic sector.

Most economists are rather zealous about preserving intact the narrow scope of economics and not soiling their hands with sociology, political science, psychology, anthropology, or history. To get too far away from the disposal of scarce goods and the allocation of resources is to risk contamination. Galbraith, like Veblen and Marx — not to speak of others who deserve mention — goes wherever an economic problem takes him, even to what a purist would call the mudholes of social psychology.

In considering the forces that have shaped Galbraith's thinking, one cannot dismiss his versatility, or, more precisely, the repercussions that versatility have had on him. Many economists have held high political office and have had access to the great of the world. Beginning with the Physiocrats and going on through the old English Classicists, the Philosophical Radicals, the Austrians, and Historicists, Keynes, Ohlin, Myrdal, and on to our own Council of Economic Advisers and Arthur F. Burns, many economists have had important posts in business and government and easy access to those who sit in the seats of the mighty from Madame de Pompadour to President Nixon. Galbraith has not only traveled widely but lived abroad for long periods. It would be tedious, bootless, and invidious to figure out which economists have been closest to the centers of power, which have been subjected to the most mind-expanding experiences after leaving the narrow — almost incestuous — academic world. It is enough to say that Galbraith stands high on the list and has visibly profited from the myriad views of life he has had. How many practitioners of economics, from François Quesnay to Paul Samuelson, would be able to dedicate a book as follows: "In memory of the President and Prime Minister who graced these years — and my life." "These years" were his years as ambassador to India and the officials were, of course, John F. Kennedy and Jawaharlal Nehru. And let us not forget that he knew, as a boy, the poor farmers of Canada.

As a postscript it is worth noting that, except for Gardner Means, he has apparently not been much influenced by other recent heterodox economists. The following are scarcely mentioned in the indices or footnotes of his books: Wesley Mitchell, John M. Clark, John A. Hobson, Rexford G. Tugwell, Clarence E. Ayres, Allan G. Gruchy, Gunnar Myrdal, Joan Robinson. This does not mean that he has not had any contact with them; I know that he has had at least some contact with Ayres, Gruchy, Myrdal, and Robinson. I also know that he has not read much of John A. Hobson, whose distinction between wealth and illth comes close to the Galbraithian phrase: "quality of life." He has also told me that he knows little about John Dewey, a philosopher who bears approximately the same relationship to holistic economics in the United States as Bentham bore to standard theory. He may, however, have learned his pragmatism or instrumentalism vicariously from Veblen, for Veblen was a devoted Deweyite. I shall have more to say about this in the last chapter.

This chapter will now trail off to a well-merited close by stating that Galbraith has *not* been influenced by the economic mathematicians; I do not remember a single diagram or equation anywhere in his work. This fact, too, will assume greater relevance in the last chapter.

CHAPTER 3

Early Economic Writings

G ALBRAITH began his professional life as an agricultural economist — rather low on the academic ladder. His doctoral dissertation, written in 1934 at the University of California in Berkeley, bore the fascinating title of "California County Expenditures, 1934." Later came an article on "Monopoly Power and Price Rigidities."[1] Now he is in the thick of it, for in 1936 the question of administered prices and rigidities was on the frontier of American economic controversy, a controversy initiated by Gardiner C. Means in 1935. A month after the article on monopoly power, he published another article, this one with J. D. Black as coauthor, "The Production Credit System of 1933."[2] This obviously goes back to his agricultural interest, for the credit system relates to farm credit. What is perhaps most interesting for us to note about these early articles is that, at the age of twenty-seven, he was already being productive in the academic sense of writing articles good enough for the learned journals. Poets may be at the height of their careers at twenty-seven, but it takes a longer time to bake, or even half-bake, an economist.

In 1938 his name appeared as the junior author on the spine of *Modern Competition and Business Policy.* The senior author was Henry S. Dennison, an American businessman well-known at the time as a manufacturer of Christmas cards, gift wrappings, gummed labels, and the like. He also had a wide reputation as a model employer and a pioneer Keynesian — at least among businessmen. With other businessmen (Morris E. Leeds, Ralph E. Flanders, Lincoln Filene) and with Galbraith, Dennison sought to commit employers to a program of full employment and reform. Dennison and Flanders published a book entitled *Toward Full Employment.* In his *Economics, Peace and Laughter* (p. 52), Galbraith writes: "I drafted it."

The Dennison-Galbraith book was published by the Oxford University Press. Galbraith seems not to be very proud of it and would willingly have it forgotten. It no longer appears in the list printed opposite the title page of his recent books under the heading: Books by John Kenneth Galbraith. Yet he concedes that it wasn't so bad as all that. Actually it is nothing to be ashamed of; indeed, it is very good if account be taken of his youth and of the times in which it was written. It popularizes the Berle-Means work on the modern corporation and makes suggestions on how mammoth companies could be controlled in the public interest. The authors do not propose the breaking up of huge firms into little ones. Here are the germs of ideas later developed in *The Affluent Society* and *The New Industrial State.* In 1973 one reads the book a little nostalgically: the only troubles they had in those days were a whopping depression with falling prices and the good, old-fashioned machinations of men like Insull. No bombing of Indochina, no unemployment accompanied by rising prices, no military-industrial complex, no nuclear devices, no minorities and busing, no Nixon or Watergate, not even witticisms by Buckley and Galbraith. There is no laughter in its 120 pages.

A series of articles on stabilization policy in wartime — later the basis of a book — were to bring him considerable notice. The first one appeared months before Pearl Harbor, but well after war in Europe had been in progress and after our own war-production program had been launched.[3] Soon after this his busy days with the Office of Price Administration began and one may reasonably suppose that he was much too busy fixing prices to write. After the war came "Reflections on Price Control"[4] and "The Disequilibrium System,"[5] both obviously relating to his work as one of the most powerful price fixers of the free world.

About this time he returned to Harvard, where his major writing has been done — either while actually there or on leave or on working vacations in Vermont or Switzerland. In 1952 his *American Capitalism: The Concept of Countervailing Power* appeared. This was the book which made his name widely known. The second word of the title is not much used by academic economists since Marx used the word contumeliously. Galbraith defends its use, however, as being descriptive and succinct. Perhaps his defense contains a hint of defiance — or panache — to his timid colleagues. The second part of the title, *The Concept of Countervailing Power,* suggests the true theme of the book. The phrase "countervailing power" (to be explained below) has become one of the widely used Galbraithian phrases, as much used as "affluent society" and "conventional wisdom."

In his preface he states that he intends to address his book to the layman despite the fact that it is not a popularization of economics. The book presents some new ideas and he hopes that these matters will be noted by the professional economist. He could have put these ideas in the jargon of economics; for he, too, he says, has the gift of writing incomprehensibly. But he wants the layman to be able to read it — though some assiduity may be required. In other words, and more bluntly than he wrote, he is going over the heads of his colleagues to present his case to a wide public. In the scholarly journals his ideas could be buried alive by learned sophists and casuists. In spite of his more urbane way of putting things, this statement of intentions must have rubbed many academic economists the wrong way. And he is at pains to state, "I think the reader will find this a good-humored book. . . . Yet this is an essay in social criticism. The task of criticism is criticism."

Roughly the first half of the book may be described as a story of the rise and fall of the competitive model — the model of Adam Smith, which holds that men, pursuing their individual selfish interests in a competitive economy, organize it for the social good, automatically, and that government should stay out of economic enterprise, except for road building, wars, and similar activities. This kind of economic system, if it ever existed, no longer lives, though it still carries on a sort of ghostly existence in the form of social nostalgia or as part of the conventional wisdom or vestigially in academic thought. It has, however, been superseded in standard economic theory by a belief in the prevalence of imperfect competition, by the belief that depression does not cure itself but needs the Keynesian remedies, and by a melancholy acceptance of the idea that government needs to intervene at more points than the Smithian model allowed. All of this is pretty heretical, yet the economy works. We are rich; to be sure there is poverty, but it is minimal. National income increases; technology improves; serious economic depression seems to be avoidable. In short, things are going well. Yet we have some vague dread of disaster. Whence comes this anxiety?

There appear to be several sources. One is a sense of guilt that we are not being true to our ideals, or, more precisely, that we are breaking the sacred economic laws of the competitive model. Second, we are afraid we may yet slip back into the slough of depression and may find that the Keynesian remedies will not work or if they do that they will subtract too much from the businessman's role as decision maker and add too much to the government's. Galbraith reassures the reader on these points. And last, we are too blind to see the emergence of a new and benevolent regulatory force, namely, countervailing power. Countervailing power tends to emerge when vast original power is possessed by an economic group. Thus when a steel trust comes into being, countervailing power tends to develop in, say, the automobile or electrical appliance industries, which purchase vast quantities of steel and, as buyers, can match their bargaining power against that of the steel oligopoly. Or, if the breakfast-food companies become overzealous in their oligopolistic pricing policies, along comes a great food-store chain which has the power — even by threatening to build its own supplying plant — to reduce exorbitant prices. It is in the interest of the chains and the automobile and appliance makers to cut their costs, lower their prices, and increase their volume of sales. This policy may not always work, since elasticity of demand and the shape of cost curves may not always permit this benign outcome — benign from the consumers' point of view. But Galbraith seems to feel that, on the whole, the consumer benefits and this process is a partial substitute for Smithian competition. It is perhaps worth noting here that the struggle implicit in this kind of competition is now waged between buyer and seller, not among a group of suppliers, as under the old competitive model.

But the development of countervailing power may take other forms. In some nations it may take the form of cooperatives; and, in democratic nations, it may take the form of subsidies or other benefits to special groups. This development explains much of the New Deal and especially the Wagner Act and farm price supports. We are not talking here about benefits to consumers but of advantages to workers and suppliers who, presumably, are denied the full value of their marginal product because of the imperfections of competition.

To be sure, countervailing power does not always spring into being or, having sprung, does not always remain effective in the public interest. It is more effective when demand is sluggish than when it is vigorous. In high prosperity, unions and industry may, despite an exchange of ancient insults across the bargaining table, combine against the consumers. In a buyers' market this could not succeed.

Thus, countervailing power can transform itself into a coalition against the public.

This theory of countervailing power suggests policy applications. It suggests that liberals should modify their notions about the effectiveness of antitrust or other stale programs of reform and should use their talents to help bring about countervailing power where such power has not been able to grow thriftily. Small contractors need protection from the overweening demands of the building trades; and migratory farm workers, from raptorial growers. This does not mean that liberals should throw away the weapon of antitrust altogether; but it does mean that another weapon is at hand.

Countervailing power should be curbed when it is used against the common good, as in a period of exuberant demand. How to do this presents a problem and we must digress for a long moment before presenting Galbraith's solution. Keynesianism is fine for combating deflation, but it is not so good for damping the inflation that accompanies strong demand. Economists generally assume that inflation is the mirror image of depression and that, when threatened by the former, all we have to do is to reverse the controls as, in a looking glass, we must raise our left hand if the reflected image is to raise its right. Perhaps this would work from a purely economic point of view, but there are difficulties. One is political. Elected officials would have to tax heavily or reduce government spending, both of which are highly unpopular. Another remedy is to reduce bank credit, but this is probably a weak remedy — a point Galbraith develops more fully in a later book; here he lets the matter stand without offering reasons for his belief. Thus, some remedy must be found which goes beyond the mere reversal of depression policy.

The book went to press in the summer of 1951; the Korean War had been successfully launched, and the pattern of the economy for the next twenty years had begun to reveal itself to the prescient: great military expenditures, the military-industrial complex, a long season of chronic but limited warfare. Such an economy, with full employment, suffers all the ill effects of countervailing power. We now get the wage-price interaction but with nothing to stop it, since no new forces are automatically set in motion to check or reverse the process. What to do? And now we return from our detour.

The only thing to do is to institute centralized decision making, which to Galbraith means governmental wage-price control. He offers this solution regretfully but feels there is no other. If the world can find peace, then inflation may not become serious enough to require control by government. An aggressive tax policy may reduce the need for detailed regulation. The dangers to capitalism are not our abandonment of the Smithian forms of competition and the existence of depression — both of which are manageable — but inflation, which invites invasive controls. On this note the book ends.

The book was variously received. Paul T. Homan, a scholar of wide understanding, gave it qualified approval. Another economist, in his review, talked a good deal about Plato, quoted several verses of Scripture, and, with Christian charity, concluded: "I should judge Dr. Galbraith one of the most effective enemies of both capitalism and democracy." This delicately worded judgment came to the attention of a senator who had previously had some doubts about Galbraith's brand of Calvinism — these were the heroic days of Joseph Raymond McCarthy. Galbraith went through some painful moments, but nothing really serious happened. Indeed, the effective enemy of capitalism and democracy got some free publicity out of the incident, which was favorable on the whole.

The economists of the land, a thundering herd, hold a roundup every year between Christmas and New Year's Eve. At one session of the 1953 roundup *American Capitalism* was the topic of discussion, and five economists gave their opinions after Galbraith had made an introductory statement. It would be tedious to discuss the observations made by this learned quintet, for they cover thirty pages and do not say very much. A few items are, however, worth noting.

Countervailing power is not reliable since it does not always spring up when and where desired and, indeed, one wonders what happened to it in the days of Haymarket, Ludlow, Homestead, and in the period when more than vasectomies were performed by unlicensed practitioners on the I.W.W. Countervailing power has a weak allocative function; it diminishes reliance on antitrust; its criteria for welfare are fuzzy; isn't Galbraith really talking about a device to relieve social tension? The theory of countervailing power does not explain the apparently eleemosynary interest which makes chain stores share the fruits of their bargaining power with their customers or take account of the fact that the low prices of the chains, with their self-service and other marketing innovations, have been able to cut costs and therefore prices. A few of these and still other objections not mentioned here would not have been made if the critics had read the book more closely and if they had noted the author's qualifications, but even economists of the first water seem to fall asleep after awhile when they read. It must be conceded, however, that Galbraith does sometimes invite this sort of criticism; he does, now and then, overstate his case. A few of the criticisms were just — something that Galbraith himself conceded. One critic entitled his paper "The Economist Plays with Blocs," a punning title which suggests that Galbraith was engaged in a child's occupation.

But "countervailing power," like Veblen's "conspicuous consumption," has become part of the language.

In the same year, 1952, he published *A Theory of Price Control.* It is a modest little book of eighty-one pages based in part on articles published five or six years earlier on price control during the Second World War (see above, p. 40). The reader will remember that, while still in his early thirties, Galbraith was one of the leading American price fixers. Now we were in a new war, though President Truman called it a police action. People, anticipating shortages, were buying ahead, or hoarding, so that they would be well supplied with coffee, salad oil, tires, and the like. Consumers' prices quickly rose by 11 percent. Friends now urged Galbraith to republish his articles of 1946 and 1947, along with a later one. He edited all three articles, added, subtracted, made changes, and adapted the texts to the new situation. The product of his labors appeared in the form of a book called *A Theory of Price Control.*

The book modestly describes itself as *A* theory rather than *The* theory because the author felt that control theory was still in its infancy; little had been written on the subject, and it was one of the expanding universes of economics. The book is not theory in the grand style with copious diagrams, coefficients of elasticity, and a snootful of parameters; it is, rather, an abstracted history of price control during the Second World War, from which Galbraith disengages useful generalizations. Some of them are negative in the sense that what was applicable to a great war engaged in by a nation all but unarmed would not be applicable to a police action engaged in by a nation with a large military force already equipped. If, besides, one believes that one police action will lead to another; that our nation, to use Paul Douglas's phrase, is a "warfare state," we cannot expect the consumer gladly to postpone consumption until the emergency is over, since the emergency is permanent and few palpable sacrifices can be demanded of consumers forever.

But the major generalization of the book is that the easiest prices and wages to control are those of oligopolies and their usually strongly organized work forces. A second and obvious generalization is that in more highly competitive markets, e.g., food and clothing, price control is more difficult and should be reinforced by an honest rationing system. By "honest" here is meant the issuance of no more ration coupons than is justified by the supply of goods. This principle was breached during the Second World War because of various political pressures on the Office of Price Administration, and price control broke down as the rationing system lost its integrity.

After the great war the American government did not keep faith. It dismantled controls too rapidly. Those millions who had saved and cooperated with the program now found their cash and bank accounts losing value at a distressing rate. The index of consumer's prices rose more than twenty percent in two years. Kicking price controls cold turkey is brutal.

The book had only modest sales. The Korean fighting ended about eighteen months after its publication. Prices remained stable for a period of five years. The years 1954, 1958, 1960 were years of depression and the problem of price control was left in the past. *A Theory of Price Control* received its fair share of reviews in the economic journals. The *American Economic Review*[6] printed a long, rambling review by an economist who wondered whether price control was better than "open inflation" and who devoted nearly a page to a form of price control which has nothing to do with war or police action, and which was advocated a year after Galbraith had finished his book. Such solitary meanderings are not unusual in the learned journals.

The two books discussed just above are quite different in theme yet reveal serious concern with the problem of inflation. And we shall find this same concern as we go on to analyze some of his later books. Inflation, for Galbraith, is not a trivial problem causing a little discomfort to senior citizens, rentiers, and schoolteachers, but a major remaining defect of capitalism. The decline of Smithian competition is often compensated for by countervailing power; depression finds its remedies in the Keynesian formulas, which do not seriously affect decentralized decision making; but inflation is a problem we have not seriously recognized or solved. It has a damaging effect not only on those whose pecuniary incomes stay level but also "on schools, colleges, welfare institutions and public services, all of peculiarly vital importance to a democracy."[7] It weakens the faith of the underlying population in government bonds. This concern shows up again in the *Affluent Society* and in his pronouncement in 1970 - 71 to the press. Before the Joint Economic Committee of the Congress, on July 20, 1971, he advocated permanent governmental controls on prices and wages. He denied the usefulness of the Keynesian remedies for inflation. This means that for thirty years Galbraith has been working on the problem of inflation. It is doubtful whether any other American economist has brooded so long or so persistently on this question.

The next book in chronological order was *The Great Crash, 1929*. It is charmingly written and Mark Van Doren is quoted as having said that it brought the language of poetry to history. Van Doren is, of course, competent to speak in this field; others may be more impressed by the book's virility of style, by its satire and ridicule. With joyous malice Galbraith tells us about the politicians and experts who, combining optimism with ignorance, were talking through their hats during the frightening months of business collapse.

As the title indicates, the book is the story of the stock-market debacle of 1929. Although all of Galbraith's economic books are easy to read — considering their content — this one is perhaps the easiest of all. It has an interesting history. It was suggested by Arthur M. Schlesinger, Jr., a friend whose name often appears in Galbraith's pages. The stock market was going up and Senator William Fulbright of the banking committee, wondering whether the new boom might be the harbinger of a new bust, asked Galbraith to testify before the committee (actually the story is more complicated, but the complications are not essential). Galbraith did testify, drawing heavily on the facts that he had marshaled for *The Great Crash, 1929*. As he spoke the stock market fell, but he did not know that. When the hearing recessed about one o'clock in the afternoon of March 8, 1955, he was met by the cameras and microphones of a broadcasting company and, released from the formality of a Senate hearing, he apparently let go, "at times grave and statesmanlike, at others perhaps a trifle flamboyant," to use his own words.[8] The market fell seven points, *(New York Times Index)* and lost three billions on the New York Stock Exchange alone. During the next few days he was inundated by telephone calls, letters, threats. A gentleman in Florida promised to kill him. To get out of it all he left Cambridge to go skiing in Vermont and broke a leg. This story got into the papers. Then he received letters from the public informing

him that there was a just God, after all. A few days later the market
went up again and, still later, his bones healed. Senator Capehart of
Indiana was displeased with Galbraith's testimony, though less so
than the homicidal gentleman in Florida. There was talk about finding out what his connection was with the gnomes of the Kremlin;
but the senator decided against pursuing the matter further, and the
incident was soon forgotten.

Part of the economic purpose of the book was to refute the widely
held belief that the stock-market crash was merely a symptom of the
underlying economic illness of the day. To state the thesis a little
differently: had there been no stock-market crash there might not
have been a depression — at least not so grotesque a decline in values
and employment. The 1920's were good years, Galbraith argues. He
does not overstate his case and concedes that some groups languished
in hopeless poverty, but this was nothing new. A flood of statistics
certified the wealth of the middle and upper income classes.
Automobile production exceeded five million vehicles, not much less
than a quarter of a century later. For many people the only danger
was belief in the law that states that what goes up must come down.

But there really was something else. The Florida land boom should
have served as a warning. It was evidence that gambling had a strong
hold on the public; or, to use the Keynesian phrase, enterprise had
become "the bubble on a whirlpool of speculation."[9] When this
happens, there is danger. The gambling kept up but was now
transferred to the Great Wall Street Casino. The speculative fever of
the gambling classes was not allayed by the leaders of business and
government or by economists — on the contrary. It is true that there
might have been a depression in 1929 - 30, but it is probable that it
could have been absorbed with only slight discomfort had it not been
preceded by the bizzare speculation of the 1920's, especially in the
last year of the decade.

Except for literary style there is something a little un-Galbraithian
about the book — at least at first reading. One misses the themes
that course through his other economic writings: quality of life, expansion of the public services, the efficiency of big business, the
weaknesses of antitrust, the nature of demand, inflation, ownership
vs. managership, and the like. Why does Galbraith interrupt this flow
of related ideas to take a flyer in American economic history? One
night conclude that economic history relaxes him — as a great
general might, in quiet and peaceful times, find pleasure in rewriting

the story of Waterloo. In briefer efforts Galbraith has written about the first Henry Ford and about the Civil War. He is a compulsive writer. What, for most of us, is an interesting idea that crosses our minds while soaking in the tub but is forgotten when toweled becomes for him an article or a book or a letter to the editor.

On second reading and deeper reflection there is perhaps a better answer. The months during the gestation of this book were months of rising prices on the stock exchange, and there was some danger that the folly of the 1920's might repeat itself in the rising generation. The return of depression was a distinct possibility. The built-in stabilizers might save us from too much pain, but, if preceded by a new speculative binge, a new deflation could again cause downright misery. Would the government again remain passive and allow the speculative orgy to develop a full head of steam? General Eisenhower was president. Would he, like his two Republican predecessors in office back in the twenties, encourage the speculators? Somebody had to sound the tocsin, and who better than Galbraith? His concern with human welfare has always been great, his opinion of Republican economic theory low. Hence this study of the dangers of speculation. Not all of this is explicitly stated, but it is there, between the lines and elsewhere.

Galbraith himself likes the book. His eyes shone as he told me (in late 1971), that it was the best written of all his books and that nobody had touched the subject since its publication. A few friendly readers — and I count myself one of them — wonder whether he really proved his point, namely, that the economy was in good shape in the late 1920's and that the stock market caused the long depression. He does, of course, concede what must be conceded: that farmers were badly off, that blacks in the South and whites in the mountains languished in hopeless poverty, that "noisome slums" were easy to find, and so on. Despite all this there was, he says, considerable prosperity, and this was true, in a way. Stuart Chase, writing just before the debacle of 1929, stated in his *Prosperity: Fact of Myth*[10] that, granting America's chronic inability to live up to its economic potential, the 1920's were indeed prosperous. But such testimony is worth very little. It was not uncharacteristic of business fluctuations before 1930 to be abrupt and discontinuous. A study of the well-known chart of business activity since 1790, published by the Cleveland Trust Company, reveals that prosperity in any given year or even quinquennium does not guarantee prosperity in the following year. Indeed, the declines in business activity appear mostly to be sudden. Paul Douglas, looking at the 1920's from the viewpoint of an oversaver or underconsumptionist, found that, during the 1920's, the purchasing power of the underlying population could not keep up with the growing supply of goods and concluded that this lag was the basic cause of the depression.[11] Depressions are probably like wars; there are fundamental causes and there is the spark that ignites: neither Fort Sumter nor Sarajevo caused the bloodletting that followed them.

In 1955, Galbraith published *Economics and the Art of Controversy*. This is a series of musing, reflective, and wondering essays about economic change. They cover only 110 pages and can be read easily. The book is perhaps the least economic of his books on economics; it does not really discuss the wisdom, unwisdom, or repercussions of economic change. It discusses, rather, the effect of reform, inspired by the New Deal primarily, on political parties, individual politicians, and durable conservatives, of whom Colonel Robert R. McCormick may be taken as a shining example. The author wonders why, when change has been widely accepted — e.g., the Wagner Act and farm price supports, to take only two cases — the shooting continues, though "with blank cartridges for ground that has already been won in a war that is over" (p. 108). Strangely enough, he observes, some reforms do not leave a turbulent wake. The creation of the social security system is one. On the other hand, impending reform, even if based on the favorable experience of other nations and closely related to what we already have done, can engender warm disputation. Health insurance is such a reform. But there is at least a chance that when this reform is adopted, controversy will subside almost completely.

Galbraith calls attention to the notoriety value of economic controversy, particularly to politicians. Except for a few gifted lawgivers in exceptional circumstances, who excel in compromise and negotiation, most reasonable politicians do not attract much notice. However by taking extreme positions, sounding the dire noise of conflict and rattling political sabers, attention and votes are attracted. And thus Galbraith goes through his little book chatting gaily, wittily, ironically about the hollowness of economic controversy and the anatomy of economic reform. The volume says a good deal about human perversity and human psychology. As has been observed in an earlier chapter, Galbraith is concerned with the psychology of economic reform rather than with the psychology of huckstering, of consumer equilibrium, of ultililty and disutility, or the other concerns of standard economic theory.

Following chronology one should take up *The Affluent Society* next, but that is a little too large a task to accomplish in this chapter. Not only is the book of major importance in the Galbraithian system but it is also a preface to an even more serious effort: *The New Industrial State.* Logic would suggest treating these in later chapters rather than zealously following chronology.

In 1960, pursuing a not unusual course for him, he gathered together some lectures he had given at Grinnell College, picked up several articles he had written for magazines, and stuck them together somehow to form a book titled *The Liberal Hour,* a mixed blessing. One of the compensations of fame is freedom to engage in the unsound practice of publishing and selling the same thing over several times, each time between different covers. The result may be interesting, entertaining, and even worth the price, but may thwart the reader's propensity to look for and find unity and congruence.

The title is a quotation from Adlai Stevenson (probably by way of James Wechsler) who so designated the period just before presidential elections, when conservatives become temporarily and expediently reconciled to liberal ideas. Later, those in Stevenson's entourage used the phrase to refer to the cocktail hour. Still later, when Galbraith introduced this phrase to his friend John Steinbeck, the latter insisted on the phrase "Milking Time."[12]

The range of *The Liberal Hour* is almost as wide as that of conversation at a large dinner party: from an excellent article on inflation to an essay, whose sole merit is that it is only mildly amusing, on the attitude of the Scotch Canadians toward the British royal family. I am a little puzzled as to why this article did not go into Galbraith's *The Scotch* instead of going into *The Liberal Hour,* but not enough to make a big issue out of it. A much better and briefer story about the royal family is to be found in his *Ambassador's Journal.* Just before going to India Galbraith went to a dinner as a guest of Henry Luce's, along with the Duke of Windsor. The Duke was telling the ambassador-designate that India would be interesting and that pigsticking in Rajasthan would be a pleasant diversion. Galbraith made polite sounds, and the Duke went on, "And you will find the people most agreeable in their own way. They have been most uncommonly decent to my niece."[13]

I have said that the book contains an excellent essay on inflation, which concludes with the standard Galbraithian remedy: wage-price controls. His view of human capital as being the most important factor of production and his plea for an educational system that will develop increasingly better human capital, appear here as they do elsewhere. In a section entitled "The Moving Finger Sticks" he demonstrates by using several examples that history often creates false but pleasing theses and myths, many of which endure as solid verities. Among them is the belief that the poverty of the American South has been caused by the Civil War. He seeks to disprove this and gives as a principal reason for meridional poverty a previously obsolescent agrarian economy. Another essay asks: "Was Ford a Fraud?" And the answer is "Yes", and that James Couzens was really the strong man in the early days of the Ford Motor Company. In one chapter, entitled "The Care and Prevention of Disasters", he returns to the 1920's, the disaster of 1929, and the appalling lack of leadership. It is a brief sequel to his book, *The Great Crash, 1929,* published three years earlier. He takes us back to the mishandling of the economy. Incompetent men were in charge, from Daniel R. Crissinger to Calvin Coolidge, with a galaxy of top-notch bunglers in between. Suicidal legislation, such as the Smoot-Hawley tariff act, was passed. There was a curious misplacing of responsibility: Hoover felt that the Governor of New York was somehow responsible for the stock-market crash, and Coolidge accepted Willian Z. Ripley's advice that regulation of the corporate machinations of the day (sometimes larcenous) was the responsibility of the individual states, not the federal government. This pleased Coolidge, for now he could relax and continue piously and laconically to do nothing. Galbraith seems to be telling us that eternal vigilance and informed federal action are the price of economic health.

One chapter on peaceful competition with Russia argues against military competition and urges that we seek respect from the world by reducing crime, unemployment, and the bad management of our cities. On the positive side we should increase aid to backward nations. We have, he notes, been generous in our foreign aid, but we seem increasingly to be supporting corrupt tyrannies, even rascals. He realizes that all this will cost money, but Galbraith believes that Americans could stand heavier taxation.

Two articles in this collection might have been written not by an economist or bureaucrat but by any beguiling essayist — say Clifton Fadiman or E. B. White — despite one unfortunate allusion to marginal and average costs. They relate to the hills and valleys of Vermont, presumably near Newfane, where he has a retreat. One of them, about how not to cultivate an abandoned farm (plant trees — don't try sheep), brought him more fan mail than any other of his short essays. In his introduction to the book, Galbraith mentions the abandoned farm essay and suggests that the Department of Agriculture should create a division devoted to relinquished land. This would, he writes, be a fitting memorial to Ezra Taft Benson "to whom all those who love abandoned farms will be forever in debt," and whom Galbraith often honors with his shafts.

We have now completed our survey of what I have arbitrarily designated as Galbraith's "Early Economic Writings". They were not all so very early, really, since he was 53 years old when *The Liberal Hour* was published. Moreover, *The Affluent Society,* subject of the next chapter, appeared when he was a little younger than that — which only goes to prove that taxonomy is an unrewarding occupation.

CHAPTER 4

The Affluent Society

*T*HE *Affluent Society*[1] is Galbraith's first great success. He was fifty when it was published. The title is not a happy one and on several occasions Galbraith has voiced *ex post facto* regrets. In popular speech and writing it has come to mean the United States, in which all are as prosperous as they are deemed to be by the uninformed and unduly patriotic. But there is a lot about American poverty in *The Affluent Society*. Actually, the book is about a society in which affluence is latent rather than developed, which has a flourishing productive system, which spreads its benefits generously, but which still has a long way to go before affluence can be enjoyed by all. The state of the industrial arts, the availability of capital, and the quality of the population make affluence possible — though not yet achieved. Galbraith's abundance must not be thought of in such vulgar terms as two Cadillacs per family, a lighted swimming pool for every backyard, a color television set in every room, and popular music piped into every nook and cranny of the house. His concept of affluence would lay stress on adequate and appropriate education for all, medical care for all, adequate food, clothing, and shelter for all, better police protection in every now-neglected precinct, better mass transportation, cleaner air and water, and other public services — all this rather than more personal possessions. He does not, on principle, object to pools and cars and television; the question is one of where to begin to increase our present but imperfect opulence.

In the early pages of *The Affluent Society* Galbraith defines a phrase that has been widely used since the book's publication: "the conventional wisdom." His explication of the phrase is a sort of clearing of the underbrush before going after the big trees. This phrase has often, like the title of the book, been misapplied in popular writing and speech. It has almost come to mean the well-worn political and economic arguments of standpatters, conservatives, and their obstinate and dated congeners. But the phrase means more. It also refers to the myths and sciolism of the radical or liberal. Neither liberals nor conservatives are or have been always wrong but much of their lore and wisdom is often founded on what existed in the past but exists no longer. Thus, Ricardo and Marx — to take polar examples — may have seen clearly in their day; but to cling to their beliefs today can be misleading, to put it mildly.

The conventional wisdom resists change and distorts our view. It is the glass through which students of society see darkly and fuzzily. Galbraith's discussion and use of the phrase "conventional wisdom" reminds one a little of Karl Mannheim's "sociology of knowledge." His epistemological introduction is a sort of warning to the reader that the author is about to challenge the conventional wisdom and that the reader, to follow him, must try to look at the society and its economy through clear glass and with a steady gaze.

From his observations on the conventional wisdom he goes on to erect a scaffolding. In four chapters he develops the concept of the economics of despair. Anglo-American economics has created a mood of hopelessness about the human condition despite the fact that the birth of economics also marks the beginning of a period in which new hope for mankind might have been found. Those who saw geometric overpopulation and only arithmetic increases in production might have been heartened by the commerical, agricultural, and industrial revolutions; but they were not. Despite the increases in productivity in store for users of better ships, of steam pumps and engines, of the spinning jenny, and of all the other things so well described nowadays in the fifth grade, the economists developed a discipline which chained the mass of mankind forever to poverty, great income inequality, and insecurity. And this is an important ingredient of the conventional wisdom. Not only that, but in the debased Darwinism of Herbert Spencer, man was pitted against man in an obscene struggle to exist; and this was considered to be in accordance with natural, if not divine, law.

There were exceptions: St. Simon and Fourier, to mention only two. But nobody paid attention to them then or later. Much more noticed, and very much at the center of attention then and now, was Marx. Although he promised heaven on earth, it was to come only after a period of purgatory. Before achieving bliss we were to have increasing poverty, longer and deeper depressions, imperialist wars,

and other kinds of catastrophes. Thus, on James Watts's 200th an-
niversary, in the midst of the Great Depression, in the year that
Keynes published his famous *General Theory*, men's minds were still
encumbered by the belief that poverty was the lot of the human race
— a few exceptions granted — and that this poverty was necessarily
accompanied by harsh competition and warfare. Economists have
done little to knock down these props of the conventional wisdom.
Some, on the contrary, have reinforced them. Over the generations
the actual situation with regard to inequality, insecurity, and low
productivity has changed enormously, but the conventional wisdom
concerning them keeps rolling along.

Productivity, or, more precisely, increased productivity, has
always been a prime economic goal and is looked upon as the ultimate answer to our economic and allied problems. Strangely
enough, though we talk a lot about the importance of increased
productivity, and though production does grow from year to year as
Topsy did, we do precious little to insure it or to maximize it — again
like Topsy. Why this neglect of what we consider to be so vital? First
of all — with a few exceptions, like the Lincoln Memorial or travel to
the moon — the only production in which we really take pride is
private production: of automobiles, mouthwashes, dog food, aircraft,
and the like. What is produced publicly is rarely a source of pride.
Moreover, public production — jails, mental hospitals, welfare of-
fices — is viewed as a burden, nay, a cross, we must bear (through
taxes) rather than as a source of satisfaction. We resent increased
costs for better education but in jocund mood pay three hundred
dollars more for a color TV set of rudimentary fidelity than for a
black and white.

We reveal our true attitude toward increased production, as con-
trasted with our professed delight, by using few of the means open to
us to expand output. We do not import labor except exiguously. We
are satisfied to allow several important industries to languish in a
state of primitiveness: coal mining, house construction, clothing, the
delivery of medical care. Thus, our reverence for production is a
pious but empty pose. We value the goods we do produce but do not
cudgel our brains to produce the goods we lack.

From such premises it is only a short step to one of Galbraith's
most controversial hypotheses, namely, that demand arises out of
production rather than the other way round. Standard economic
theory, it will be remembered, holds to the hypothesis that demand

comes first; then, after the demand is sensed somehow by the entrepreneur, he responds to it by producing the desired good. With Galbraith production comes first; then the producer creates or contrives the wants that result in purchase by the consumer. The creation of wants is achieved through advertising and allied arts. Wants depend not on the untutored desires of man, but "on the process by which they are satisfied."[2] The product comes first; then the producer moves heaven and earth to sell it. Galbraith does not hold this to be true of all goods; wholesome foods and fluids are, of course, untutored wants, though it must be observed that even these have a wide range and that wants for what may be considered primitive foods, such as monkey stew, worms, human flesh, can be contrived or annulled, if not by Madison Avenue, then by priests, shamans, or Druids. This reversed analysis of demand he names the "Dependence Effect."

If this is a true analysis of demand, we shall have to concede that much of our vaunted production is mere boondoggling, that consumers would be equally happy if they consumed only a fraction of what they do consume. To be sure, the problem of unemployment would then arise; and, since this is so, we must ask ourselves whether we employ workers to satisfy our wants or whether we expand our wants just to keep people at work. At this point a problem of values intrudes. What kind of production is boondoggling and what kind is "truly" productive. Galbraith does not face the problem head-on, but it is clear that some things are one and some the other. What is noisy, crude, dirty, unsightly, vulgar, dangerous, tawdry is boondoggle; good medical care for all, decent mass transportation, rat-free housing, aesthetic rural and urban vistas are examples of the opposite. Standard theory tries to keep away from value judgments, but it fails, though it thinks it succeeds. Jeremy Bentham set the tone by saying that "quantity of pleasure being equal, push-pin is as good as poetry." This in itself is a whopping value judgment, but standard theory still cites it as a nonvaluational dictum. It has been used against Galbraith by some unidentified economist, quoted by Paul Samuelson.[3]

When wants are so contrived that they will induce consumption of privately produced goods, two dangers appear: first, the instability (boom-bust) that may arise from installment buying and second, the danger of inflation. The first of these dangers Galbraith discusses briefly in more or less conventional fashion; thus explication is not needed here. The second, inflation, requires a few words. Rising prices are an affliction of the affluent society, even in peacetime. The cures, or mitigations, of standard economic theory are high interest rates or increased taxation, widely known as monetary policy and fiscal policy, respectively. The first pleases conservatives and the second pleases liberals, and neither of them works. He analyzes the reasons for their failure (see below); whether his analysis is right or wrong, the irrefragable fact is that after decades of trial they have both failed. Even so irreproachable a Republican as President Nixon noted this and established direct wage-price controls in 1971.

High interest rates place restraints on borrowing, inhibit entrepreneurial investment, and shrink consumer purchasing — at least this is the conventional wisdom. Galbraith does not agree. In the affluent society of mammoth corporations, high interest rates are mere pinpricks — at least to the mammoths. They can borrow directly from the public if the banks are obstinate, and they can, usually, raise their prices to maintain the profits to which they feel they are justly entitled. In short, a high rate, unless "applied with severity over time," will not bother the large corporations very much. Small firms, however, such as farms, residential building companies, and the like will feel the pressure; for they must borrow at the bank — or try to — and they cannot adjust prices upward, as large monopoloid firms can. The considerable political influence of countless farmers and small businessmen must, however, be reckoned with. As for the consumer who buys on time, Galbraith argues, a 33-1/3 percent increase in the interest rate will, typically, increase the monthly payment by about 3 percent, and even this can be offset by lengthening the term of payment or can be made to seem painless by various obfuscations carefully thought out by the intellectual Ajaxes of commerce.

Will not fiscal policy do better than monetary policy? When fiscal policy has been adopted, the underlying population is made to pay higher taxes or the government's public expenditure programs are reduced. Thus, demand for goods and services is reduced and prices — so it is said — will go down and inflation will go away. From the purely economic point of view this seems to be an infallible remedy; but there are political difficulties.

The underlying population does not joyfully pay higher taxes when prices are rising and consumers are already feeling the crunch of high prices. And now, to restore the consumers' purchasing power, we tax him more heavily. Politically, this is not a good way to remain in office. Complicating this is the perennial issue of whose taxes should go up. The liberals try to protect the lower-income groups; the conservatives try to protect the higher-income groups. The results of this conflict do not provide an optimum solution or a reduction of class tensions.

As for reducing expenditures, observation tells us that governments simply do not reduce outlays, regardless of the good intentions expressed by executives and legislators. The logic behind this failure is not too clear, but one may surmise that every claimant or pressure group holds that its expenditures are sacrosanct and that some other group should be satisfied with a reduced appropriation. The net result is no reduction of spending, at best; at worst, a considerable increase.

In passing, let us take note of the fact that here Glabraith introduces a political argument at a point where politics is not often introduced by economists. True elegance in economic reasoning, so highly prized by the purists, rules out evidence from the other and less pure social sciences.[4]

Thus we are doomed to have inflation so long as we rely on our present lore to combat it. As before, Galbraith prescribes wage-price-profit control; but in this book, written in 1958, he believes it is politically unacceptable. Thirteen years later, President Nixon did institute such controls, feebly, to be sure.

The emphasis we place on production to meet contrived wants leads not only to instability and inflation, as we have seen above, but also to unbalanced production. By unbalanced production Galbraith means primarily the disparity between our high achievement in the realm of privately produced goods and services and our low achievement in the realm of publicly produced goods and services. Here occurs the now celebrated passage about the vacationing family in their mauve and cerise automobile, fitted with the usual options, filled with packaged foods and drinks in the car refrigerator, which must drive through littered streets, past unsightly dumps and junk piles, with views cut off by billboards explaining halitosis and acid indigestion, and which must finally spend the night in an unsanitary park near a polluted stream, where they sleep on their luxurious air mattresses. This is an absence of "social balance."

In the days of Adam Smith it was reasonable to argue that the public authority should stay out of the production of goods and services except those related to courts of law, defense of the realm, and such few indispensable engineering projects as could yield no profit to the man of business. Much of our standard theory and conventional wisdom is rooted in the theory of those days. But those days are over. Great contributions to our happiness could be made in these times by an expansion of the public services. We do not understand how much we need certain public services because nobody clearly explains their merits to us, as the makers of — say Lavoris — explain to us how we can and should perfume our gingivas and uvulas with their mouthwash. The government not only does little to create wants but also responds slowly to wants that already exist. Thus, traffic control, reasonably priced medical care, pollution control, crime prevention, pleasant vistas, and a few Roman piazzas scattered about in our cities are not wanted with the same urgency as privately produced goods for which wants are created by expert psychologists, excellent commercial artists, clever poetasters, and dingdong composers. Those who invent new private wants are honored citizens; but a "politician or public servant who dreams up a new public service is a wastrel. Few public offenses are more reprehensible."[5]

The provision of abundant public services would have favorable ramifications that are not immediately seen. Let us look at the favorable effects on housing: decent housing depends not only on decent buildings but also on good city planning, prompt collection of trash and garbage, streets filled with light, general cleanliness, well-paid policemen, open spaces nearby, traffic control, and so on. Without these the decent buildings with which we started can easily become slums and often do. The advantages of a good educational system are well understood from the viewpoint of the individual, but the wide-rippling benefits to the society as a whole are less well understood. Childless married couples who complain about paying a school tax should try to imagine what our society and economy would be like if illiteracy were rife.

The neglect of the public services, which is the chief cause of social imbalance, arises in part from our unwillingness to open up the question of inequality of income, and from the tendency to inflation. Galbraith seems to feel that, although palpable economic inequality of reward does exist, the issue is quiescent in an affluent society. Though citizens generally benefit from expanded social services, the benefits to the poor are more highly visible; and although all pay for them, the per capita payment by the rich is usually greater than by the poor, and this fact is trumpeted up and down the land. Enough friction results to lead to inaction.

In a society with chronic inflation those who perform public services are among those least likely to maintain their purchasing power by wage and salary increases. The more alert and competent candidates for such jobs seek work elsewhere. Thus performance and productivity are low and deteriorating. And, Glabraith might have added, the temptation to accept bribes is great, particularly in the case of those engaged in the administration of criminal justice. All of this tends to lower the esteem in which the public services are held.

Education is a means of improving human capital but, because it depends largely on the public services, it is slighted. Research is equally slighted. Production, the professed aim of the society, is held down in volume, variety, and excellence. And this reluctance to spend for education affects our society through the channels of consumption as well as production. Our consumers are literate enough to consume obediently but not literate enough to consume with discrimination. It is easy enough to stimulate gross wants in the bosoms of unlettered people, such as wants for automobiles, television, deep-fried potatoes, hamburgers, catsup, and pornography. It is harder to implant in them a desire for travel or *boeuf bourguignonne* (which costs scarcely more to make at home than hamburgers). It is easier to make complusive shutterbugs out of our fellow citizens than discriminating photographers. Singing commercials are not used to stimulate the development of such hobbies as hybridizing peonies or delphiniums — inexpensive but rewarding hobbies. Demand for good theater does not arise from those who are drugged with *Hogan's Heroes* or even *I Love Lucy*. Diversification of consumption and resistance to the banal would help to stabilize the economy in perhaps the same way that a diversified portfolio stabilizes the income of the private investor.

In what we may now call Galbraith's model of the economy, we see a society still anxious about our ability to produce, many decades after the resistance of nature to affluence has been reduced in importance. Thus we go in for excessive and irrational production which, however, is limited to the sphere of privately produced goods. Advertising and allied arts make us obedient but undiscriminating consumers of these goods. We think we want them because we are told to want them. A society so organized endangers itself through instability and inflation and brings on unemployment. An affluent society is held together tenuously and courts disruption. Are there any remedies?

The first remedial step demands that we give up our long and deeply ingrained feelings about the virtues of work. Much of our work is meaningless, anyhow, because much of what it produces meets only contrived needs. When Adam delved and Eve span and Ruth gleaned in the fields of Boaz, every grain of wheat was precious. Now we give the stuff away. Toil was indeed important then, and even the minority that could avoid arduous labor felt compelled to classify its activity as work: warfare, exorcism, government, the search for arcana. A slothful species would probably not have survived.

But things have changed. A smaller fraction of the human race needs to work. Unemployment, shorter hours, the virtual exclusion of teenagers from the labor force — all demonstrate to us that unremitting toil is not necessary in an affluent society. Besides, much of what we do produce might as well have been left unproduced. Yet the disesteem attached to the nonworker persists; or, to be more nearly accurate, we still feel strongly that he who does not work should not consume any part of the social product unless subjected to degradation.

Our economy seems to demand unemployment; yet those on whom this hardship falls are stigmatized. If we could believe that they also serve who only stand and wait, we could, in our hearts, divorce income from production. That is the first step; the next is to improve our present system of unemployment compensation. It is niggardly in amount and brief in duration. Galbraith proposes that we remedy these two faults and suggests a new feature: the size of the benefit should be related to the total number of unemployed. When the total number is small, the compensation should be small; when large, the benefit should increase — increase close to the average wage (or previous wage). This scheme could be superimposed by the federal government on the variegated systems of the individual states. That there may be cheating when compensation moves close to the prevailing wage is conceded, but Galbraith does not seem to be much worried about the relatively small leakages we may have. He is a *de minimis non curat praetor* sort of guy.

A second remedy to insure the improvement and persistence of our endangered society is to redress the balance between the private and public sector. A major question here is who should pay. Galbraith's answer is paradoxical and characteristically original. He suggests a general sales tax. I have talked to many economists about this, and they unanimously oppose this method of financing. It is almost an axiom of economic theory that a general sales tax falls with greater force on the poor than on the rich, whereas the public services are generally deemed to benefit the poor more than the rich. Thus, in essence, Galbraith seems to be saying, "Let the poor pay for their own social services." And, to many, this practice may seem unjust or, at least, callous. Actually his proposal is more humane that that. He would argue in favor of his proposal as follows:

1. The middle and upper income classes favor sales taxes over income taxes; if we wait for income-tax reform, we shall wait indefinitely for needed public services — and the hour is late.
2. Although there are indeed poor people in the affluent society, few are in the deep poverty of the developing nations; what should not be done there can be done here.
3. Moving forward now without too much debate on the financing of the public services is more important than trying to solve the ancient problem of inequitable income distribution.
4. The sales-tax method of financing the public services will make the commodities of the private economy more expensive, which is a good thing, since we need fewer of them anyhow.
5. The public services will, in the long run, do more to alleviate poverty than excusing the poor — especially the hereditary poor — from taxation; they will get better housing, better health care, better education, cheaper transportation, and so on; this policy is better than letting them spend a few dollars more on cola drinks, patented breakfast foods, cigarettes, hair-and mouth-rinses, and the other privately produced trivialities of an affluent society.

The three terminal chapters of *The Affluent Society* leave this reader with the impression that Galbraith had already finished the book some twenty-five pages back but wanted to add some observations allied to his main themes. He notes that, contrary to widespread belief, productive capacity is not directly related to military might. A comparison of the U.S. and the U.S.S.R. would support this thesis. This is one way of saying that we erroneously place vast emphasis on productive capacity, partly because we feel that the nation that can produce in greatest volume can most efficiently trample on the foe. More important than voluminous creation of goods and more useful for survival is scientific advance through education. Galbraith has unshakable confidence in education. Since he knows how easily education can become pedantry or conventional wisdom or the presumptions and misconceptions against which Francis Bacon inveighed more than three centuries ago it is rather remarkable that his faith is so great. Perhaps someday he will write a book on educational aims, for education is much too important a matter to be left to educators.

In one of his terminal chapters he makes an interesting observation concerning the development of a new class in our society and with it a diminution of the human costs of labor. This is reminiscent of J. A. Hobson's discussion of the same problem in his *Work and Wealth*.[6] Standard economics usually considers all work to be homogeneous and to be a disutility, and that the only reward is the pecuniary reward. Occasionally it does point out that artistic or scientific work is more agreeable than collecting garbage, but it leaves this observation dangling. Galbraith points out that in the affluent society more and more varieties of work are taking on the aspects of artistic, scientific, and professional work, and that those who perform labor of this sort may be named the New Class. He gives examples charily but presumably the new class would include such workers as paramedical practitioners and highly specialized teachers (of the deaf, blind, mentally retarded); in any case, the spread of education and the progress of science would open up new and interesting careers, ones that are intrinsically rewarding, though a pecuniary reward is also obviously needed. Since we may look forward to the virtual abolition of stoop labor, monotonous work, and back-breaking toil, the society will be happier.

I felt on reading this section that this disquisition on a New Class satisfied two wishes of Galbraith's: first, that the affluent society, without radical change — for Galbraith is no revolutionist — held within it the possibility of achieving the Utopian goal of producing goods and services without ignoble toil and second, that of rebuking standard theorists for their basic Benthamite assumption that work was a pain that could be counterbalanced only by the pleasure of consumption.

He ends his book with the following:

To have failed to solve the problem of producing goods would have been to continue man in his oldest and most grievous misfortune. But to fail to see that we have solved it and to fail to proceed thence to the next task would be fully as tragic.

Since *The Affluent Society* and *The New Industrial State* have numerous points of similarity and elicited similar criticisms, I shall discuss the reception and evaluation of both books in the next chapter.

CHAPTER 5

The New Industrial State

IN 1967 Galbraith published the first edition of his now famous *The New Industrial State*. The foundations of the book had been laid in *The Affluent Society*, but it has much more to say about the economy and the society than the earlier book. The world first became aware of the argument of *The New Industrial State* through six (Reith) lectures given by Galbraith over the BBC and printed in *The Listener* during November and December of 1966. That argument can be summarized rapidly if the assumption is made that the reader has already absorbed the thesis of *The Affluent Society*.

In *The New Industrial State*, he treats of only part — let's call it half — of the economy. That half is of the great or "mature" corporations. Quantitatively these corporations may be more or less than half of the economy, depending on the criteria used. To Galbraith, however, they are much more than half partly because they define the trend toward which the economy is moving and partly because they affect our culture as a whole more profoundly than the competitive section composed of millions of small firms.

Just as Adam Smith and Marx gave us great models of the economy, so Galbraith gives us a grand model of his economic world, or half world. The work, to paraphrase an article on Galbraith by Brigitte Lépine and Jacques de Douhet, is of wide scope. It evokes those problems of the industrial world that bother us most: growth, consumption, alienation, management and bureaucracy, the military-industrial complex, convergence of East and West, great corporations, and the future of the postindustrial world. Even this is not an exhaustive inventory.[1] The book had sold more than a million copies by August of 1971.[2] This number includes translations. It most certainly has circled the globe at about the 42nd parallel north, probably less completely at the level of Africa and South America.

The Japanese made a big fuss over it. It succeeded "as well in Christendom as heathenesse."

The summary to be given below will draw on both the original and revised editions. The true governing body of each gigantic corporation is a "technostructure," that is, a group of managers, scientists, and other highly trained persons working together as a committee. The board of directors and stockholders are of minor importance and hardly bother the technostructure at all. The latter has virtual control over the prices of its products; and, because it can hold on to a large fraction of the corporation's profits, it does not depend exclusively on banks for expansion — it can flow back the profits withheld. Much of this is accepted by most standard economists. But now Galbraith goes on to say things that are less acceptable to them.

Mature corporations, he says, seek profits, of course, but not to maximize them. This leaves the technostructure with the possibility of achieving aims that are, in standard theory, undefined. What other aims do they have? The chief one is growth. They do not respond to consumers; consumers respond to them — indeed are subject to them. This inverted sequence is made possible by advertising and related crafts. Galbraith thus dethrones the consumer and holds consumer sovereignty — a pillar of standard theory — to be a mere myth. The consumer is, in fact, brainwashed and compelled to buy what the corporation is willing to offer. What mammoth corporations cannot provide or do not wish to supply we do not get. This is a form of planning. To quote from the second Reith lecture: "When . . . [the initiative] passes to the producer — and when the consumer is accommodated to the needs and convenience of the producer — it is commonly and correctly said that we have a planned economy." This statement will get him into trouble later, as we shall see.

The investment of mature corporations in physical capital is so great that they cannot take chances on any serious faltering of demand. They therefore support government in its policies to maintain purchasing power at a high level. But their liaison with government is even closer than this suggests. They want government as a customer, not only for the profit they make on sales but also because government tends to subsidize research; in weaponry, space travel, and nuclear power. This research also benefits civilian production and, all in all, cuts down corporation research and its considerable costs. In contrast to the smaller firm, or, more precisely, the firm that still harbors an identifiable entrepreneur, the technostructure is not hostile to governmental intervention — though exceptions are conceded.

The first aim of any technostructure is, of course, to survive, and survival means that it must make a minimum profit. The second aim of the firm is growth, largely financed by undistributed profit. Maximization of profit is not important; for one thing, the technostructure is a salaried group and cannot, like the entrepreneur of the immature firm, gain much from increased profit. Great size does probably have a large effect on salary, perquisites, prestige, patronage, and, perhaps, nepotism. The stockholder must, of course, be kept at bay, but he does not amount to much. Some economists have disputed this. The millions of stockholders who own a few dozen shares can, of course, be neglected. But the man or family that owns ten million dollars' worth of stock may have much to say, even if ownership on such a scale represents only one percent of the value of all stock.

Other aims of the gargantuan firm are discretionary, such as excellence of product, aid to education, or presentation of great TV dramas instead of *The Untouchables*. At any rate it need not aim at the simple entrepreneurial goal of maximizing profits, which is the putative terminal point as seen by standard theory.

The technostructure is a new factor of production and is becoming more nearly essential in the process of turning out goods. Under feudalism, land was the basic factor of production; under early capitalism, land and the landed gentry declined in importance and the owner of capital came to the fore. Labor's power never counted for much, but with trade unionism it increased in importance. Now the technostructure is the most important factor.

The increasing symbiosis between the technostructure and government is revealed in part by the interchangeability of personnel. The late "Electric Charlie" Wilson slid in and out of government office; George Strange McNamara, a business executive, filled a governmernt job close to the president's in importance; flocks of military officers go into private business. This situation may require a new theory of government, but Galbraith denies that it is proof of the Marxian theory that the state is the executive committee of capitalism. Neither is it fulfillment of the Schumpeterian predictions. To see things either way is to iterate the conventional wisdom. We are no longer dealing with capitalism but with the technostructure, which is something new in the economy.

The technostructure has its roots in the development of science and technology. By science and technology Galbraith means more than physics and chemistry and their applications; he also means psychology, sociology, methods of accounting, statistics, and anything else that may be used to increase production and reliably to create wants. Wherever the technostructure has developed, it takes charge. This is true even of the Soviet Union. The tendency toward convergence of the two economic systems — capitalist and socialist — results from the fact that their technostructures demand the same things as ours. Rebellious youth is turning away from Russia and toward China and Cuba because these nations have not yet been taken over by technostructures; when they are, the luster they now have will tarnish for them.

Galbraith does have a theory of the state in this book. In the heyday of the entrepreneurial corporation men "of subtle mind agreed with Marx that the state was or would become the executive committee of capitalist enterprise."[3] Business control of the state was then the thing to fear. The entrepreneur of those days, either alone or with a family or very small group, owned the corporation and had access to corporate funds, which could be used to bribe individual politicians, or for that matter, whole state legislatures. He had a strong interest in getting concessions from government since any superprofit that accrued to him from his backstairs political activities, belonged to him and those near and dear to him. The mature corporation with its salaried technostructure has much less interest in turning over a specific sum to buy a specific benefit. Moreover and again, any benefit that increases a corporation's profit does not accrue to an individual entrepreneur or limited circle of owners. Nevertheless, the mature corporation does want some benefits from the government. It wants national growth, trained manpower, the regulation of aggregate demand, reasonable stability of wages and prices, scientific and technical advance, and defense. These are also the goals of the state. Thus many private goals merge with public goals. The technostructure thus becomes an extension of the governmental bureaucracy. This theory, if verifiable, would demonstrate that convergence between the United States and the Soviet Union is inescapable. The technostructure is a thing unto itself, and governments — wherever and whatever they may be — must adapt themselves to it. This fact does not mean however that the technostructure will be unbending; accommodation is a two-way affair.

The priorities of the technostructure determine the priorities of the society as a whole. Education, art, worthy use of leisure, peace, comfortable and economical mass transport, decent housing and medical care for all, clean air and water, noiseless machines, clean streets, safe and pleasant parks — none of these has much interest to the technostructure; hence are largely ignored by the underlying population. To express a desire for them is to be eccentric, Utopian, Idealistic, and even subversive. A man of standing is a jocund captive of the technostructure and a submissive consumer of what is offered.

Is there no way of saving ourselves from the technostructure? Perhaps not, but there is some hope. The technostructure, we have said, has become the most important factor of production. It has become dependent on what Galbraith calls "the educational and scientific estate" for its supply of very highly trained manpower. The values of this "estate" are not those of the technostructure, though massive exceptions occur. Standard economists adapt themselves easily to its goals. But many university students and teachers do not; they feel a growing tension between themselves and this new factor of production. Individualism is still highly valued by students of the classics, humanities, and of some of the social sciences. Clergymen, writers, actors, musicians, and even athletes contribute to this group of latter-day disestablishmentarians. A confrontation between such groups and the government occurred in 1967 - 68 over Vietnam, which resulted in President Johnson's retiring from politics. This kind of response may suggest a pattern for the future.

The book was revised and updated in 1971, but the changes were not great. Perhaps the major change was that, in the second edition, Galbraith clarifies his use of the word "planning." When he used the word in the first edition it was not clear whether he was talking about the planning of the gargantuan firm or about the overall economic planning of an entire economy. He was talking about the gargantuan firm, which must make sure of its raw materials, working force, and demand months or even years before it proceeds very far in its production. This effort requires planning, especially when sales of each of the fifty largest companies exceed two billions a year, and more than half of them exceed three billions. The book was most successful, as I have said, and girdled the globe in many translations. Standard economists in the United States paid it the compliment of long and scholarly reviews and of assigning it to their more formidable practitioners for disemboweling.

Before we go on to examine reviews and oher appraisals of *The*

New Industrial State and *The Affluent Society,* a few general observations must be made. They will serve as a sort of guide to Galbraithian criticism. First, it should be noted that noneconomists usually praise him. They are enchanted with his style, satire, irony, social criticism, and say little about his economics. Standard economists, however, tend to disagree with his economic message, and their criticism goes from civil disagreement to uncivilized revilement.

Second, *The New Industrial State* was the sixteenth of a series of books produced over a period of three decades, mostly about economics or some branch of the social sciences. It was apparently looked upon as a swan song; for Galbriath, though still exuding health and expending much energy, was no longer a cygnet when it appeared. Thus, some of the important reviews of the book also probed backward into what might be termed "The Galbraithian System," and paid retrospective attention to several earlier books, particularly to *The Affluent Society,* which did lay the foundation for *The New Industrial State* and it formed a system of sorts.

Third, most reviews are as banal as the books they evaluate and most scholarly books are banal. Galbraith's are not and reviewers rise to the occasion with impuissant incandescence, which ranges from attacks on the man himself to eloquent restatements of the conventional wisdom. The attacks *ad hominem* sometimes scrape the bottom of the barrel. Let us look at the more delightful scrapings: Galbraith writes English too well to be a good scholar; when he utters nonsense the stock market falls; he mingles with the Beautiful People and may be a Beautiful Person himself and therefore is a poor economist; he is a big thinker and little thinkers make better economists; he does much of his writing in Gstaad, and something is vaguely wrong about that; his writing is fretwork; he often sneers; he arouses envy in other economists which is not good; he is rich and therefore his marginal product is too great and therefore, also, he has no compassion for the poor.

A few criticisms, though still in an area of doubtfully good taste, are more justifiable. One is that through his pellucid prose he goes directly to the layman with his new theories instead of filtering them through the journals and subjecting them to the prior evaluation of his colleagues. This criticism is sanctioned by the tradition — even the ethics — of other branches of scholarship, where positive harm might be done by premature popularization. If a physician should develop the theory that sauerkraut juice is a prophylactic and cure for migraine and get his message over to the average citizen without its being certified by other medical men, much harm might be done and a woeful misallocation of sauerkraut might be the result. But economic changes and reform cannot normally be implemented by individuals. Legislation is usually needed and this means hearings and logrolling and bribes and lobbying and crippling amendments and riders. All this fortunately allows for plenty of time to assess the soundness of the proposed reform.

Another frequent criticism is that he says nothing new. It has all been said before by Veblen, by J. M. Clark, by Keynes (in his essay on the economic possibilities for our grandchildren),[4] by Alvin Hansen. This criticism may be true in the loose sense that there is nothing new under the sun or even that there is nothing new except what has been forgotten, as Marie Antoinette's milliner put it. I spoke to two of Galbraith's old teachers at the University of California, and they defended him with the argument that much of what has been said before needs to be said anew. It is certainly true that Galbraith does not rank with the great innovating minds of the world — at least not yet — not with Newton, Adam Smith, Darwin, Freud; and it is true that one recognizes in his work the influence of Veblen and others, and one wishes he would give them a little more credit. But he is original, and he has hacked away at one problem, at least, namely inflation, with more zeal than most other modern economists. To say that *The Affluent Society* and *The New Industrial State* are nothing but warmed-over Veblen or Hansen or Keynes is to downgrade him maliciously or ignorantly, or both.

Galbraith is also accused of carelessness, exaggeration, vast generalization, and unsupported statement. His friends and admirers tend to overlook these tendencies as peccadillos, whereas his enemies look upon them as sins. However one may wish to describe these faults, one does get the feeling that he is sometimes not thorough enough. Two instances, one small and one large, will clarify the nature of the accusations. Somewhere he says that soon after Veblen's writings on conspicuous consumption, property values in Newport fell precipitously, implying a cause and effect sequence. This is nonsense. It is doubtful whether the leisure class, to this day, knows the difference between Veblen and a hole in the ground. A more important instance is his writing *The New Industrial State* without clarifying the distinction between national economic planning and the planning of an individual firm. In the revised edition he corrects this error, as I have stated above.

Some of the criticism of Galbraith, even if addressed to genuine economic issues, is trivial. For example, when discussing the large corporations' retained earnings he says they are "an overwhelmingly important source of capital."[5] Robert M. Solow, in an unfriendly review, presents several inconclusive figures to show that Galbraith is wrong, but then concedes that self-finance is "an important aspect of modern industrial life."[6] One wonders how significant the difference is between one man's "overwhelmingly important" and another man's "important." Another critic attacks belief in the power of advertising to shape demand by stating that *he* is not influenced much by advertising. This is proof by introspection, which is not widely accepted in scientific circles. It sounds too much like almost everybody's dogmatic Aunt Priscilla.

On their side standard economists do have a few real grievances. Galbraith sometimes attacks standard theorists with his not inconsiderable arsenal of literary weapons, from irony to pity and from dysphemism to oxymoron. He scolds them for not listening to him and tells them that they avoid his truth for fear of losing the prestige they have achieved through their mastery of economic scholasticism — Veblen called it theology. Such accusations, prepared *ex ante* and *ex animo,* are maddening enough to make a normal standard theorist accuse Galbraith of making too much money, of being a Beautiful Person who associates with the Beautiful People, and of trampling on the poor.

When Galbraith attacks a central principle of standard theory he arouses vast resentment, but when he accuses its defenders of clinging to their principles because they will lose their rank in the profession he is insufferable. But there is more. As a once prominent civil servant, a successful writer, and a semishowman who gets on television fairly often he cannot be ignored. There are plenty of economists who, like Galbraith, question the principles of standard economic theory. But they are little gray moths and can be easily disregarded by the elite, the chosen people, who run the dismal science. Galbraith cannot be neglected. He is perhaps the most readable and formidable economist who ever lived. It is easy to be jealous of him.

Some of the fiercest fighting between Galbraith and his critics revolves around the concepts named "The Dependence Effect" and "The Revised Sequence."[7] These relate to the theory that many wants are contrived, mostly by advertising. Standard theory holds that human wants have no limit and that entrepreneurs find out what these wants are and try to satisfy them. The origin of these wants is immaterial and their urgency is not measurable. Who is to say that food satisfies a more urgent want than a mouth organ?

Under this theory the consumer is king and his slaves — General Motors, General Electric, General Foods, IBM, ITT — are breathlessly waiting for a sign from him as to what his wants are. Galbraith holds, roughly, to the opposite view, namely, that wants, unless contrived, are not extravagantly large; that the consumer is servile; that, with exceptions, the mammoth firm succeeds in creating demands for its products; and that wants can be ranged in order of urgency. All four of these statements are more or less offensive to proponents of standard theory, but the last one really makes their blood boil. It introduces the contaminating valuational note that changes economics from a "pure" science to a discipline that allows ethical judgments to intrude. Wants cannot be ranged in order of urgency, say the purists. Standard theory does, of course, recognize a few exceptions. Heroin, Saturday-night specials, gold bullion, and certain other commodities are not legally available on the free market either because they are intrinsically forms of illth or, in the case of gold, because free buying and selling would disrupt international trade as now organized. But, a few obvious exceptions conceded, economists have no business fooling around with the concept of more or less urgent wants. Wants are wants, as we find them on the marketplace, and the business of the entrepreneur is to supply them, whether tutored or untutored, original or contrived, essential or trivial.

The fountainhead of untutored demand is indeed well concealed from our eyes. Demand in the aggregate is a product of the interaction of basic human, even protoplasmic, needs with history, culture, propensity to emulate, geography, myth, nationalism, scientific discovery (vitamins), advertising, and aggressive propensities, to mention a few evocative factors. A child in his crib reaches for the shiny object; a housewife reaches, apparently, for the most brightly colored box of dried prunes or detergent; the youth for the motorcycle with the most murderous look. Experience has proved to grocers and commercial bakers of bread that customers will most often buy the brand that is piled highest on the shelf. The anthropologist wonders about the forces that cause rapid or slow diffusion of culture. The use of tobacco in Europe after its discovery in America spread with amazing rapidity but without boy-and-girl commercials. The clothing industry is decentralized, yet certain styles in women's clothes — the halter, miniskirt, pants suit, bikini — catch on quickly without a technostructure. Popular but evanescent songs can be heard in the same month all over the great cities of the world as if blared out from a universal loudspeaker.

To search for untutored, uncontrived demand is as hopeless as to search for "original" human nature. It is doubtful that Galbraith is trying to separate "original" from "contrived" wants. What he is saying is that a vast number of our wants is contrived by the technostructure and that this is an unsatisfactory agency for the shaping of demand, particularly since the technostructure is not equipped to supply adequately certain important needs such as delivery of health care, low-cost housing, or an aesthetic environment. To take full advantage of our vast productivity (affluence), other agencies must stimulate or supply other wants and these agencies do not exist. But even beyond that he is saying that we live in a topsy-turvy sort of economy in which the very process of satisfying wants becomes a process of creating new and even needless wants, that much of our production is wasteful, a form of boondoggling, a method of sustaining employment. And there is nothing sacred about employment.

On the whole economists who specialize in industrial organization do not like what Galbraith has to say, and he apparently has little use for them. Joe Bain, Walter Adams, John Blair, and other distinguished specialists in industrial organization disagree sharply with Galbraith. One of them said to me, "I don't know why Galbraith won't read our books." They believe that he ignores the amount of competition that actually exists or that could be made to exist if pressure were applied. They deplore his informing his many readers that the mature corporation is an inevitable result of a highly developed technology, that huge firms are more efficient than small ones and that they are the major innovators in our economy. Obviously, by "small firms" they do not mean only cabinetmakers or custom shoemakers, with a few helpers. They also mean firms of about the size of Milton Bradley, Oneida Ltd. (silver), Remington Arms, Bulova Watch. Such firms are large enough to enjoy economies of mass production, but they do not attain the elephantine proportions of General Motors, Exxon, and others of their approximate magnitude. It is not quite clear why Galbraith does not try to respond directly to the observation that small firms are successful in improving technology and their products, but a few possible responses come to mind. First, whatever the small firm may have done in the past, its day is over. We are moving toward the economy of mature corporations and we must consider what they can do, not what the obsolete firms have been able to do heretofore. And the mature corporation is doing a tolerable job, to say the least, of introducing new processes and products. Second, the day of atomistic competition is also over. To seek to recapture it is to be as hopelessly out of line as to seek to bring back the watch fob and the hoopskirt. Third, basic research and innovation have gone beyond the stage of working on relatively simple mechanical problems, such as are involved in the split-ring notebook or the self-starter for the automobile or the variable-pitch propellor for the airplane. Significant research today requires a whole company of men and women — few of them necessarily gifted — who are at home inside the atom and the gene, and who can call on the services of geologists, physicians, and other specialists. Only the vast corporations in their symbiotic relations with government can afford to do this sort of research.

In holding to this view Galbraith has recently gained support from his colleague Daniel Bell, the sociologist. In his book *The Coming of Post Industrial Society,* Bell writes of nineteenth-century industries that were created by "talented tinkerers" who knew little about science. Innovations today do not depend on the flashes of genius of such men as the Wright brothers, Ford, Bessemer, Ericsson, Bell, and Morse. Modern industry depends on basic science, not on gifted mechanics or nineteenth-century chemists.

The industrial economists also contend that the colossal firms are not the inevitable outgrowth of technological development but result from sins of omission and commission on the part of government and from the greed, ambition, and wrongdoing of a few businessmen. Here we are partly in the realm of psychology and partly in the realm of determinism. Standard theory assumes that, barring exceptions, men compete honestly, within the rules of God and man. The exceptions should be indicted, tried and thrown into dungeons. Galbraith has a less exalted view of mankind and probably believes there are not enough dungeons to go round. This is not to say that human beings are base, depraved, vicious, or incapable of sublimity. It does mean that men do not like to compete in the honorable way that neoclassical economists think they do or should. As for technological determinism, the question is: does technology induce people to behave differently from the way they would if the technology were not there? The answer is certainly yes. I have already, in Chapter 2, spoken of the influence of the automobile on sexual morality. If one can accept this argument, then one should not find it hard to accept the argument that technology affects our methods of production, our attitude towards the size of a firm, towards the benefits of competition, and, to skip the intermediate steps, towards our whole outlook on life.

Objections were made to *The Affluent Society* and its successor to the effect that even in the most highly developed societies the problem of production has not yet been conquered. F. A. Hayek, one of the ablest nineteenth-century economists still professing his science in the twentieth, criticizes Galbraith on this issue.[8] He describes the idea as an old socialistic idea, dating from Saint-Simon (1760 - 1825) and persisting into the present. It is not clear whether the antiquity of the idea is *prima facie* proof of error or of Galbraith's incompetence. Some obtuse persons might think antiquity to be irrelevant or even corroborative. Equally inconclusive was an article in *Fortune,* which asks the same question in a backhanded way, "Are We Too Rich Already?"[9] Without giving a real answer to the question whether we produce too much, too little, or exactly the right amount, the article seems to agree with Galbraith. It does argue however, that Americans do not consume wastefully. This statement is of course open to question. It is an old saying that Europe could live on what America wastes — though Europe has perhaps changed that in the last quarter century. *Fortune* concedes that American taste is not always of the best, but the article ends on the hopeful note that, given time, it may improve without governmental prodding. The review also regrets that Galbraith did not clearly point out that American business has caused American affluence.

Obviously we shall never produce enough of everything for everybody; and if we did, some of the products would no longer be desirable. If every woman could buy a gallon of Chanel No. 5 every week, the scent would lend no distinction to its user and would lose most of its present utility, and the solar system would reek. If every American family wanted and could have a seaside cottage on the coastline of the United States each owner would get approximately a ten-foot frontage, a figure that would make life by the sea an abomination. It is very difficult now, and will always be difficult, to find a great wine of the Médoc, thirty years old and still getting better; and certainly there are not enough wines of equal quality for every American family for every Sunday dinner. Many things such as truffles and caviar will long have to be rationed by price or otherwise, despite the marvels of technology. But one must not downgrade technological possibilities. Seventy years ago only a few lucky people heard Caruso or saw Sarah Bernhardt. If these artists were alive today, the hi-fi and the camera could bring them to us and to posterity almost as in life. If, however, we think of our capacity to produce cabbage and kohlrabi, ham and hamburger, chicken and chowder, the question of undercapacity vanishes. Housing remains troublesome; but someday the unholy trinity of contractors, politicians, and the building-trades unions will have to be broken up, and new dwellings will then flourish; besides, more "good addresses" — or tolerable addresses, at least — can easily be created if we do something about mugging, street lighting, and restraining automobiles from thundering along on the level of our second-floor windows — or simply restraining automobiles.

The question of what is adequate cannot be answered by the literal or childlike mind. Through science, legislation, and international cooperation Americans have virtually abolished smallpox and the fear of it. This boon increases our living standard more than would possession of rubies and mink by all. Aggregate production and personal wealth should always be viewed against the standard of living of the times and be divorced from myth and fairy tales. The concept of personal wealth today is not very much different from the concept of wealth held by Scheherazade or the dairy farmer of *Fiddler on the Roof.* It is still pleasant, like him, to daydream about wealth in obsolete terms: many loyal servants, sable, ermine, half a dozen residences equipped with fountains and marble halls, at least one palatial yacht, dozens of lovers, hunting preserves, and thoroughbred horses. All this belongs in the realm of the immature and even vulgar mind. Psychologically, wealth conceived in these terms harks back to the infant's sense of omnipotence. It is not necessary, when committing suicide, to take the posion of powdered diamond, as did the Rajput chieftain's daughter, Rupmanti.[10] For most of us ground glass would do.

We must conclude then, that when Galbraith writes about the adequacy of production he is not saying that we produce enough to realize the daydreams of infantile minds. He obviously means production that will give to everybody basic food, clothing, shelter, medical care, reasonably safe and comfortable public transportation, and education appropriate to the capacity of the person being educated. The economy should also offer some amenities: whiskey, gin, baseball, football, the cinema, television, books, tennis, fishing, canoeing, swimming, playing cards, music, painting, and the other modest pleasures of a democratic and cultivated society. It is obvious that we cannot have even these things while we allow all other things to remain equal. Decent transportation would, for example, probably require curtailing the use of the private automobile and switching the resources it uses up to public transportation. It might mean the breakdown of several professions into paraprofessions. And it would certainly mean cleaning up air and water and reducing noise. But to doubt that we have the technology to provide something more than frugal comfort for all Americans is to be ill-informed.

It should be made clear that Galbraith does not say all the things that have been said in the last few pages, and he might disagree with specific items. But it is also clear that anybody who reads him with imagination would say things not too different from what I have just said.

Several of Galbraith's critics disagreed with the statement that the vast companies do not maximize profits. Actually, many standard economists do agree but often with qualifications or by professing this belief for the record and then ignoring it and its consequences — a time-honored tool of economic analysis that dates back to Ricardo[11] or earlier. It simplifies economic theory if one admits only one aim, profit maximization. It accords, moreover, with the behavior of the economic man, which is a basic preconception of standard theory. Galbraith, of course, concedes what is elementary, namely, that profits are primary in the sense that no firm, not even a gargantuan one, can survive without profits (or some reasonable substitute, such as a bounty), but after minimal profits the firm — or, rather, the technostructure — usually seeks growth. The technostructure is not a group of entrepreneurs; they cannot appropriate profits; their situation individually resembles that of a bureaucrat in government, who increases his prestige and salary by empire building. Standard theorists can reply by arguing that whether profit is used to recompense the technostructure or to contribute toward growth is a matter of small importance. In either case money is being avidly pursued and economic reasoning is not changed. Most of the good old diagrams and models and things remain the same. Galbraith's counterargument is that it makes a lot of difference to the economy if profits are used for expansion and for other miscellaneous aims instead of for enhanced personal income, and that difference is one subject of his study.

In France *The New Industrial State* was received with much interest and, at least in two influential publications, with more sympathy than in the United States. *Paris-Match,* similar to our now defunct *Life,* gave him an effusive welcome in its issue of December 4, 1971. He had the lead article, an almost life-sized camera portrait, flanked by pictures of Adam Smith, Malthus, Jackie Onassis, McLuhan, and Marcuse. The last two were the other great American thinkers; Jackie was the symbol of Galbraith's relationship to the late President. The whole thing looked like *mardi gras,* or maybe the midway at the state fair. The burden of the article and its garish embellishments was that Galbraith was neither a standard nor Marxian economist, but rather he had found a new interpretation of capitalism and its further drift.

His reception by *Le Nouvel Observateur* of Paris was a much more dignified and scholarly affair.[12] Galbraith spoke in Paris under the journal's auspices on February 2, 1971. The auditors were apparently readers and friends of the publication, which is left of center. He was introduced by Pierre Mendès-France, economist, lawyer, and former premier of France. He was followed by three speakers who, in the elegant jargon of American scholarly conferences, would be called "discussants." Two berated him for his unwillingness to go Marxian, whole-hog, since some of his theses accorded with those of Marx. Galbraith replied — to be brief — that Marx and Lenin did not live to see the technostructure in its present form and might have written differently if they had lived; that the U.S.S.R. has a bureaucracy similar to the technostructure and follows its dictates rather than those of Marx. Social change, he thinks, comes not through the efforts of a proletariat, as Marx predicted, but through the efforts of a wider group of the disaffected. Elsewhere, in several places, he speaks of himself as favoring evolutionary rather than revolutionary change.

The same issue contains an article by Brigitte Lépine and Jacques de Douhet, who devote nearly thirty pages to the subject of Galbraith and his critics. Much of what they have to say under Galbraith's economic theses we have already covered above. However, they do additionally note that such American Marxists as Paul Sweezy and Paul Baran as well as Michel Rocard of France believe that the technostructure forms part of the apparatus of good, old-fashioned capitalism. Paul Sweezy may note with approval, they say, Galbraith's emphasis on the military-industrial complex as a customer; but he deplores Galbraith's omission of the subject of foreign markets and exploitation of the third world , that is to say, imperialism.

Perhaps of greater interest to Americans is the Lépine-de Douhẹt discussion of the socio-political theses of Galbraith. The two French writers find Galbraith to be, if not in the mainstream of American thought, at least in a strong crosscurrent. He carries on his work in the tradition of James Burnham, C. Wright Mills, William H. Whyte, David Riesman, Vance Packard, Ralph Nader, Herbert Marcuse, and even of the novelist Norman Mailer. They also recall Aldous Huxley's predictions in *Brave New World* of methodical conditioning, techniques of manipulation and felicific tranquilizing by chemistry. Obviously they refer to Galbraith's obedient consumer, drugged by advertisements — not by chemicals, yet.

From economics we now turn to other writings of Galbraith's — from art to political romance, more like Voltaire's *Candide* or Anatole France's *Isle of Penguins* than like a treatise on economics.

CHAPTER 6

Noneconomic Writings

BOTH Veblen and Galbraith have written much outside the immediate realm of economics. Veblen translated and interpreted the (Icelandic) *Laxdaela Saga*. He wrote about a Viking captain of industry whose sense of business enterprise was precociously developed for the century thereof. He discussed the intellectual preeminence of the Jews, Christian morals, and a variety of other subjects generally considered remote from economics. Galbraith also discusses things that have little to do with economics: the mighty research of a fabled Dr. McLandress, the trials of a fictive Latin-American country in the throes of revolution and the greater trials of the U.S. State Department during the revolution, the hollow and ritualistic nature of economic controversy, public architecture, the limited talents of the first Henry Ford, and much more. And one asks: why did these two economists go off on these tangents? Perhaps because both are gifted humanists of wingspread too great to be contained by the small cage of economics. One can, of course, specialize and specialize and specialize in economics or engage in busy speculation from the lower rungs of scholasticism; but if such activities seem to be vain, other employments must be found. A born satirist can spray neoclassical economics too easily and quickly with his buckshot and must find other things to spray: mankind, for instance.

We begin our survey of the noneconomic writings with *The McLandress Dimension,* which first appeared under the pseudonym of Mark Epernay[1] — Mark for Mark Twain and Epernay for the town in Champagne that had figured in a book Galbraith was then reading about the Franco-Prussian War, while ambassador to India. That will give the reader an idea of how ambassadors spend their time. Well, anyhow, Mark Epernay (or J.K.G.) is the Boswell of Dr. Herschel McLandress, a paragon among psychometricians. The book is amusing foolishness based on rock-ribbed truth. James

Stevenson's drawings enliven an already lively book. It reminds one of the discussions of Parkinson's law and similar satires — for example, the one about kicking people upstairs just beyond their true abilities.

One of the learned doctor's investigations related to the length of time a person could keep his mind focused on things other than himself — this was named a "coefficient." The late Dr. Oppenheimer had a coefficient of three hours and thirty minutes, while Dr. Edward Teller had a coefficient of about three minutes, approximately equal to Elizabeth Taylor's. James Reston, Truman Capote, Dean Acheson, Vladimir Nabokov are all ten-minute men, give or take a little. Although the size of the coefficient is proclaimed to be value-free in the sense that a two-minute man is no better or worse than a two-hour man, still, it is interesting to note that most of the men and women whom Galbraith admires seem to have larger coefficients than those he does not admire or admires less.

One must, of course, establish these coefficients with care and mother wit. Take, for example, the case of that famous native of Lorraine: General de Gaulle. His case was puzzling, for his coefficient was a whopping seven and a half hours. Recalculated, however, to take account of the fact that the great general could not tell the difference between himself and all of France, the true coefficient turns out to be ninety seconds. The reader will see how much fun psychometry can be and how, through this science, one can say things about people that, said otherwise, might lay one open to unpleasant legal action.

Dr. McLandress realizes that half-rich men are at a considerable disadvantage as compared with really rich men, particularly in one area, and seeks to redress this handicap. The truly rich can afford foundations, which not only keep them informed in the right way but also tell them what to say in after-dinner speeches, at ground-breaking ceremonies, at dedications of buildings, and when interviewed. Under the condition that formerly prevailed a half-rich man could not really speak intelligently about China because he could not afford a foundation; but with the aid of the McLandress service he can now say as snobbily as any Rockefeller brother: "We should eventually recognize China, but in the meantime the Chinese must give up aggression, recognize Formosa, conciliate Asia and approach the free nations with clean hands."[2] No foundation could do better. Sometimes, depending on the issue, the McLandress reply is con-

ceived in the womb of "overlapping moderation," which may turn
into contradiction; for example, "An arms race endangers the survival of mankind: As a practical matter, however, we cannot give up
our deterrent force." Sometimes the best way to answer a difficult
and embarrasing question is to select a "third dimension departure,"
such as: we must appoint a high-level, gold medal, task force to
analyze the political, economic, military questions involved, and
their repercussions.

The chapter named "The American Sociometric Peerage," after
noting that the American system of class distinction, or social
precedence, is extremely complex, describes an objective, infallible,
and mathematical method worked out by the ineffable Dr. McLandress to put each person in his proper pigeonhole. Since real names
are used, this chapter, like the first, gives Galbraith the opportunity
to rib friend and smite foe — and sometimes to go a little beyond
that.

"The Confidence Machine," subject of another chapter, is well
summarized by Galbraith himself in his *Ambassador's Journal,* page
349: "This was a machine which, by playing recorded speeches of
Herbert Hoover and Barry Goldwater in a subdued hum was
designed to sustain the confidence of business executives." The
machine was so miniaturized and transistorized and otherwise improved that it could be hung, unseen, under the shirt and could hum
messages of confidence twenty-four hours a day.

The book is fun to read. Here, even more than elsewhere in
Galbraith's prose, the full flavor of the humor will be enjoyed only by
those who are "in" or who follow the "in" people faithfully, whereas
the ordinary man — like myself — or the pedagogue or the Ph.D. in
economics is sometimes a little annoyed that he does not see the joke;
but the book is still fun. It reveals Galbraith's world partly as
follows: the State Department is an ass, except for "Chip" Bohlen.[3]
The businessmen respond perversely to exhortation; rather than
seeking, in depression, a cure, they want to hear the troglodytic
hosannahs to a free market, individual initiative, and pre-Keynesian
doctrine of a Herbert Hoover, Calvin Coolidge, Barry Goldwater.
The United States, contrary to the children's textbooks, does have an
aristocracy but is only now beginning to identify it. Knowledge of
basic things is rare, and what passes as knowledge is puffed out, gas-
eous, and pretentious. He sideswipes all sorts of sacred things: conferences with their "workshops," "discussants," "seminars," foun-

dations with their timid scholarship, and the British royal family, except for the photographer fellow.

From the great Dr. McLandress we go to the book named *Indian Painting*. With Mohinder Singh Randhawa, Galbraith published, in 1968, a charming, elegant, and expensive book of 142 quarto pages with thirty-four color plates and sixteen black and white illustrations, the latter mostly of architectural subjects.[4] It is beautifully done and probably is among the better coffeetable Christmas presents. About half the color plates reproduce Indian paintings of the eighteenth century; the remainder begin at A.D. 1600. The preface suggests that Randhawa got hold of history, stories, and legends illustrated by the color plates and that Galbraith converted this into chastened prose. One sees, here and there, evidence of Galbraith's mischievous style; but here he has no ogres to fight, no standard theorists to scold, no paperwork bureaucrats in State to snap at, no Vietnam war to deplore. Thus the book has a quiet, even-tempered charm. Although not widely reviewed, it was, deservedly, well reviewed. The book is another example of Galbraith's versatility and industriousness; it testifies to his genuine interest in art.

In 1964, *The Scotch* appeared in book form, parts of it having appeared earlier in *Harper's Magazine*. The word "Scotch," applied to people rather than liquor, was acceptable — indeed mandatory — on the northern shore of Lake Erie. The book is a collection of memoirs rather than an autobiography. He, himself, speaks of it as "an exercise in social anthropology," and this is a good description, though I prefer my own description: a retrospective and informal socio-economic survey. The period covered is roughly between 1910 - 1925, the years of Galbraith's childhood and adolescence. The book is as nostalgic as a 1910 Sears Roebuck catalog. There were few automobiles and no snowmobiles, changes of long underwear were infrequent, winters were cold, baths and adultery rare, drinking monosexual and spasmodic, though deep and even violent when it did occur. Cutters were still used on the unploughed snows. Frugality was one of the primary virtues in this quasiegalitarian community. There were several churches but Calvinism of some sort covered them all. The Protestant ethic ruled.

A few shafts are directed at modern Americans, among them John Foster Dulles and Ezra Taft Benson, neither of whom is ever mentioned by Galbraith — here or elsewhere — in a spirit of comradely affection. Once his father, who made numerous political speeches, mounted a manure pile to speak — presumably no other elevation was near at hand — and began by apologizing for appearing on his opponents' platform. This was brilliant wit, and there was much laughter. His father, however, later told his son that the sally was good but that it had not changed any votes. Galbraith remembered this in the years of Adlai Stevenson's unsuccessful but witty campaigns. One surmises that Galbraith, who supplied some of the wit, recalled his father's wise observations but that the temptation to be funny was too strong.

The book, as I have said, is not autobiography; therefore certain things should not be expected of it. Nonetheless I rather missed certain standard autobiographical touches: sucking icy mittens; freezing the tongue on frozen skate blades; attacking the bully; longing, at eight, to row across Lake Erie to Put in Bay; fantasizing in adolescence what the girl in his Chapter 3 would do if he, Kenneth, were to waste away and die.

He says, in *The Scotch* that in adolescence he read a book by Anatole France which modified his hitherto Calvinistic views on unhallowed love. At times he writes enough like Anatole France to make one wonder whether he did not read many books by the Frenchman and whether the irony had not entered his soul. But he could not have learned much about autobiography, for the little Pierre Nozière was more engaging than the little Ken.

The next book to consider in this group of noneconomic writings is *The Triumph,* published in 1968. This revenge on Dean Rusk is as sustained as was Voltaire's revenge on Leibnitz in *Candide.* The whole is a political romance. One of the best descriptions of the book is contained in a review written by Robert Brown and printed in the *New Republic.*[5]

Brown states, "What Galbraith is concerned to demonstrate is the system of interlocking stupidity in which, he believes, the makers of foreign policy are hopelessly imprisoned."

Like some of the chapters of *The McLandress Dimension,* it attacks the bureaucracy of the State Department with witty malevolence and occasional violence. The plot, basically, is about the handling or mishandling of a fictional revolution in Latin America by our State Department. Not all of the shafts — and there are hundreds — are directed at Foggy Bottom. The old and new governments of the imaginary country, Puerto de los Santos, a sugarcane and coffee nation, receive their share of venomous arrows.

The laziness, cynicism, graft, machismo, intrigue, whoring, duplicity, nepotism, and corruption of the Latin American officials make them rather unattractive persons.

Galbraith's principal character and major target is Dr. Grant Worthing Campbell, an assistant secretary of state. He is an over-cautious man and a stuffed shirt but not an object of ridicule. He is, in his limited way, intelligent, even-tempered, seemingly tolerant, apparently willing with his closed mind to see both sides of every debatable issue. His major defect is that in reality he sees only what Galbraith here and elsewhere names "bureaucratic truth." The gulf between bureaucratic truth and real truth is wide and deep. Bureaucratic truth comes into existence through policy fixation, or arrest, at some time in the past — somewhere around 1950 for the United States, when Red China and the Soviet Union seemed to form a threatening Communist coalition and Senator Joseph R. McCarthy was in his prime. Campbell's mission in life is to protect the State Department from policy changes, from truth as revealed by events. He is able and knows how to deal with people. And, of course, the policy is to prevent the minuscule revolution in the miniscule coffee and sugar nation from becoming a majuscule Communist takeover of the world. In the end the unperceptive men of Washington achieve precisely what they tried so hard and pitifully to avert, namely a Communist dictatorship for Puerto de los Santos. The cream of the jest is that the new left-wing dictator, educated at the University of Michigan, is the son of the former fascist, or, rather, gangsterlike, dictator.

Next we take up the *Ambassador's Journal,* 1969. All of Galbraith's books are serious; for Galbraith is a serious man, but this book is also relatively sober — but only relatively so. He deals with many exalted personages, many of whom he likes and admires, and with events that demand sober treatment. To be sure, the Department of State and its bureaucrats are not accorded undue respect, and the tone of self-mockery is persistent. His exile, if such it was, is relieved by frequent journeys back to the United States, to Hong Kong, Japan, Switzerland, Indochina, Bethesda Naval Hospital, not to mention excursions to the more enchanting parts of India itself.

The book has little to do with economics, though he drops many casual observations on economic matters, some directed at American policy and some at that of underdeveloped nations, but nothing is reasoned out fully. The book should, however, be of interest to political scientists, historians and to foreign-service officers. It tells you all you ever wanted to know about how an embassy is run, what its relations with Washington are, perquisites, out of pocket expenses, the making of policy, the tensions between the man on the scene and the man at the desk in Washington. The footnotes, identifying persons, buildings, rivers, lakes, jokes, diseases, citing elevations of mountains, explaining American slang that might be offensive to Indians — all this is a work of art. The index is twenty-one double-columned pages long and lists the names of perhaps seven hundred persons, with many of whom he had some contact either in India or the United States. Too many of these, I feel, are referred to as "friend," "good friend" and even "devoted friend." If ever I should have the opportunity to turn a psychoanalyst loose on him, I think I should introduce this friend business as primary evidence of a minor ailment, at least. It is also interesting to note what names are not mentioned at all, not only here but elsewhere, as I propose to point out later. However, for the moment, I will note that George Meany, John Dunlop, H. J. Reuss, I. Lubin, Harry Bridges, are not mentioned. It is, of course, quite probable that none of these men had anything remotely to do with India. But many other people in the book also had nothing to do with India. Leaving this aside until the last chapter, we may marvel at the number of businessmen and bureaucrats who went to India on some pretext or other, often wholly or partially at the taxpayers' expense (the businessmen presumably making tax-deductible trips), not to mention show people, journalists, authors of note, and Milton Friedman, all of whom Galbraith had to be nice to. There were plenty of problems and plenty of turmoil during his service in India: Red China's shooting of people, the beginning of Vietnam, Kashmir, Goa, and so on; but the task was not one to rend the heart as was — let us say — John Winant's tour in London during the Second World War.

The book ends with touchingly understated sadness that the Kennedy years were over. One cannot help speculating on what would have happened to Galbraith had Kennedy lived. He might, like W. Averell Harriman, have become a free spirit in international politics, handling a variety of delicate jobs. He might have been a sort of Harry Hopkins, but without the gift of self-effacement. I wonder, in the spring of 1973, whether he would have wanted Kissinger's job, and whether he now envies his Harvard colleague. I feel he would have liked to be Secretary of State. I do not see him in an elected office — as Senator from Massachusetts, let us say. I'm afraid that he would, like his father, have mounted a dunghill, apologized for using Nixon's platform, and lost the election.

I do not think he would have been much interested in the Secretaryship of the Treasury, since the job offered no real challenge — at least this was true of that post until 1972, when it was converted by Richard Nixon into something else. And the chairmanship of the Council of Economic Advisers just doesn't seem to be very Galbraithian; its occupant is too much desk-bound. One speculates on what would happen if, in 1976, a Democrat should win and name him Secretary of Defense. Perhaps only Galbraith could now write the story of what would probably happen — and what a delightful story that would be.

Galbraith also wrote three tracts for the times between 1967 and 1970. All three are "How To" books in the sense that they are addressed to concerned voters or to voters who should be concerned, and all three urge specific action in what were then proximate presidential and congressional elections. All three were eventually published as "Broadsides" by the New American Library under the following titles, subtitles and blurbs:

1. *How to Get Out of Vietnam* (1967). The war we cannot win, should not wish to win, are not winning. The assumed enemy does not exist.
2. *How to Control The Military* (1969).
3. *A Lucid Proposal for The Nation* (1970). Who needs the Democrats and what it takes to be needed.

All three foreshadow positions taken by Senators Eugene McCarthy and George McGovern in the 1968 and 1972 presidential campaigns. In 1971 I asked Galbraith whether these Broadsides were continuing publications and whether one might expect a new Broadside soon. His reply was that he had felt deeply about the subjects when he wrote the ones discussed above and that, whenever he again felt deeply about something, he would write another. None have appeared. It is now mid-1973, and nothing of significance has come from his pen about Watergate.

He also wrote a little book in 1973 on Communist China. This was a short book on his brief visit there earlier in the same year. It received indifferent reviews and was not widely noted.

CHAPTER 7

Economics and the Public Purpose

*E*CONOMICS *and the Public Purpose* came out two years after this book was started and just about the time it was due to be sent to the publisher. Had Galbraith's book appeared a year ago, it might have changed the structure of this book a little, though not much, and I beg the reader's forgiveness that the inclusion of a summary of the new book is added to, rather than integrated with, the remainder of the text. If this chapter is too long and contains redundancies, my excuse is that, like Pascal, "I lack the time to make it shorter."[1]

Economics and the Public Purpose is the most complete book he has written on economics. It reminds one — though rather vaguely — of the great "Principles" and "Grundriss" books that appeared between the days of John Stuart Mill and Frank A. Fetter. They were intended to cover all the important concepts of economics but were not always comprehensive. Marshall's famous *Principles* said almost nothing about foreign trade or business cycles. Something necrotic happened to such books during the Second World War — probably because of the confusion caused by the depression and by Keynes and by the world's absorption in slaughter. The nearest we have come to a new, definitive book of "Principles" in standard theory is Samuelson's ubiquitous textbook, entitled simply *Economics*. But it is just a textbook, full of what he calls "parables" and of schoolmarmish humor designed, apparently, to amuse and instruct the posthebetics.

The dissidents, too, were producing their "Principles." Marx's *Das Kapital* told us more than many of us wanted to know. Veblen's *Theory of Business Enterprise* was a reasonably complete book and so was John Hobson's *Work and Wealth*. Now at long last another reasonably complete heterodox book has appeared, Galbraith's *Economics and the Public Purpose*.[2] Almost every basic idea

Galbraith has put forward about economics in the last quarter century appears in this book but often in slightly different form or context. This book integrates his part work. It is a chemical compound of old elements, not a physical mixture. One senses that an unconsciously teleological process has been going on in Galbraith's mind which culminates in this volume.

Economics and the Public Purpose is divided into two major parts: (1) an analysis or description of the economic world and (2) the theory of reform, which suggests how to change that none-too-pretty world into a better one.

The description, analysis, or model is partly founded on *The New Industrial State.* Half the model consists of the great firms which, with their vast power, control selling prices, buying prices, demand for their product, and strongly influence the belief system of the culture. Each firm is controlled by a bureaucracy, which is usually called a "technostructure," and which has been described in an earlier chapter. This part of the economy, composed of about one thousand firms, Galbraith names "the planning system," because it is adept at planning its buying and selling prices, the amount produced and sold. These firms — also sometimes called "the mature firms" — are virtually independent of their directors and stockholders, because they are, at best, only part-time supervisors and rarely possess the technical skills demanded by the firm. Control is in the hands of the technostructure.

In all this there is nothing new. What is new is the attention Galbraith pays to millions of firms in the other part of the economy. This part he names "the market system," because it has not shaken off and probably cannot shake off governance by the forces of supply and demand. This is the residue of nineteenth-century capitalism, with entrepreneurs, small stores, laundries, restaurants, repair shops, costermongers, fishmongers, entrepreneurs of funereal pomp as the French so beautifully put it, other small operators, and — Galbraith rarely forgets them — hookers and denizens of the bordello. There are few trade unions in this sector. Exploitation of employees is still common, and self-exploitation is rife, as in the case of the momma, poppa, and Rosie stores that stay open every day until 10 p.m.

The rewards to those populating the market system are generally lower than those received by the planning system, though exceptions must be conceded: successful artists from Picasso to Agatha Christie do as well as corporation magnates; and here and there others in a variety of fields do very well indeed. Small incomes compared with those of the moguls of the planning system are, however, the rule. On the other hand, this inequality is bearable because the members of the market system enjoy a psychic income which Galbraith names "the convenient social virtue." This cachet is a little like the Protestant ethic, and that is why it is a "social virtue." It is "convenient" not to the possessor of the virtue but to somebody else, usually the planning system or, in another situation, to the male chauvinist pig whose wife is his servant. The overworked farmer is rewarded by the fact that he is considered a sturdy yeoman, the backbone of America; and the local ironmonger may be rewarded by membership in Kiwanis and may even "see John Knox in paradise." The market system may be and is exploited by the planning system because it is weak and lacks bargaining power.

The market system is not, as Marxists may say, a transient or laggard system destined to perish as its members are taken over by large firms or destroyed by the onward march of technology. It is here to stay. One of the aims of public policy should be to increase the power of the market system, if necessary at the expense of the planning system. Here Galbraith harks back to the prescription he gave in *American Capitalism,* where he discussed countervailing power; yet, curiously enough, he makes no mention of that book or even of countervailing power in these pages.

He would also cut back the power of the mastodonic firm. But, except as an auxiliary engine, he would not use the antitrust laws to achieve this end. We have had the legislation for some eighty years (not to mention preceding centuries of common law); but the yield has been low. They have not prevented the growth of the business giants. Just as one cannot catch buzzards and eagles by putting salt on their tails, so one cannot do much to the Goliaths with antitrust. Anyhow, the aim of returning to a competitive society is contrary to the *Zeitgeist.*

A third element in the compound that we name "the economy" is government. To Galbraith the state is an essential feature of the economy, not something to be ignored as it is in standard theory. Of course, the state is not really ignored, but it is not integrated into standard theory; or, at best, its role is dimly perceived. Speaking broadly, the state has a function in what the orthodox name "macroeconomics," but not in what they fondly call "microeconomics." This distinction Galbraith finds to be without merit. Half the economy, the planning system, "exists in the closest association with the state."[3] The core of this relationship is the role of the government as purchaser of arms, airplanes, cement for roads, autos, trucks, and the like. The state pays for much research and innovation, for the education needed to produce trained manpower, for the measures needed to sustain general demand, for aid to transport by air, land, and water, for bailing out such companies as Lockheed. The technostructures of companies in the planning system resemble governmental bureaucracies, and all bureaucracies have a tendency to understand one another and to work together to achieve their aims, which are often identical or at least similar. The notorious example is, of course, the Pentagon and the arms industry. Even the regulatory agencies come to understand the industries they regulate so well that they often forget to regulate them in the public interest. Legislatures have lost much of their original power and often take their cues from the bureaucracies.

The planning system tends to seek aid primarily from the bureaucracies and only secondarily from the legislatures. The market system, on the other hand, finding the bureaucracies unresponsive to its needs, goes to the relatively feeble Congress. Thus its wants or needs are feebly met. The legislature is made weaker still because it harbors members who are captives of the bureaucracy. "Powerful" members of the two houses are usually men who have the backing of a bureaucracy — of State, the Pentagon, Agriculture, Commerce, Transport, whatever. They are the veterans with much seniority.

The market system's approach to Congress is only mildly productive. Thus the thousand firms of the planning system get much more from government than the millions of firms in the market system. Galbraith sums it up: "The modern state, we may remind ourselves once more, is not the executive committee of the bourgeoisie but it *is* more nearly the executive committee of the technostructure."[4]

The above, then, is the model of the economy: a powerful planning system, a weak market system, and a government that responds actively to the desires of the former and less actively to those of the latter.

Much of the above is a clear outgrowth of his previous major books and articles on economics, but a few new ideas are introduced and a new mood creeps in. The new mood is an increasingly bitter assault on standard theory. He has for many years made harsh judgments against the orthodox, but now he really hectors them.

Their response should bring forth some delightful prose during 1974, when the learned journals carry reviews of his latest book.

The second innovation is his treatment of the woman question. Woman, as Bebel and Veblen have observed, is a cryptoservant. Veblen assigned to her the role of consuming conspicuously for her master. Galbraith updates him in the modern idiom. Galbraith gives woman the further task of consuming voluminously. The idea seems to be that if women were not kept at home by our culture, they would consume fewer of the useless things that flow in increasing volume from the planning system. If women worked or were encouraged to spend their time in worthy activities, they would have less time to see and hear advertisements, to stock the home with dust-catchers and other worthless objects. The planning system has no sympathy for womens' lib, because it would find fewer customers for its often useless products. Presumably the girls would read *Consumer Reports* rather than the beautiful and persuasive ads in both pulps and slicks. Given the existence of a full-time consumer in each normal family the planning system can safely produce and sell a vast quantity of stuff whose principal function is to be cared for — washed, shined, and polished. A modest three-course dinner for six with cocktails, wine, and liqueurs will require about 160 items that must be soiled and then cleaned. The planning system will resist attempts by women to get jobs — good jobs — outside the home and will continue to proclaim as particularly virtuous the women who stay at home. Indeed, the sense of being virtuous through her captivity is one of woman's chief rewards for being the "cryptoservant" that she is.

His third addition is his theory of international trade — or, at least, his observations on the subject. He ignores entirely the elegant Ricardian-corn-law doctrine of comparative advantage. He ignores the equally elegant equilibrating effects of gold movements or changes in national income. Instead, he goes directly to the phenomenon of the multinational corporation, seeking in its extensions overseas an explanation of the problems of foreign trade. Philippe de Seynes, an Under-Secretary-General of the United Nations, has noted, as has Galbraith, that "international production generated by multinational corporations has surpassed trade as the vehicle of international economic exchange."[5] This fact becomes the starting place for theorizing, not the process of taking goods to a frontier, crossing it, and then selling the goods for what they will bring.

Multinational firms, such as I.B.M., General Motors, Nestlé, are part of the planning system. As we have seen, a major aim of the planning system is to keep every possible variable under control and in achieving this aim these firms have much success domestically. But in foreign trade uncertainty bulks large unless something is done about it. And the planning system does do something about it. By re-creating itself in foreign lands the mature corporation can operate on equal terms with its competitors, that is, join the foreign oligopoly. Thus Opel, alter ego of General Motors in Germany, is circumspect about clashing in mutually disastrous competition with Mercedes and Volkswagen; and they, in turn, behave punctiliously in the American Market.

What has just been described is the situation among mature corporations and mature nations. Advanced nations seek raw materials in underdeveloped nations; the latter are subject to the market or to the superior power of the mature corporations. Either way, the sellers of the underdeveloped lands get a rooking, and the whole arrangement perpetuates inequality of income. The above compresses what Galbraith also compresses, but enough has been said to suggest his approach to the topic and to conclude that the benefits of foreign trade, as promised by standard theory, are uncertain.

At this point Galbraith ends the first part of his book and is almost ready to go on to the subject of reform, which constitutes the last third of the book. But he stops here for a breather before going on. In this section he first points out that lasting instability (depression or inflation) results primarily from the carryings-on of the planning system and then overflows to the market system. He does not deny that boom and bust existed in the days before the planning system was well developed — before 1914, let us say. But presumably the instability was brief, self-correcting, and not very painful. One wonders a little about the mid-1870's in the United States, the unemployment noted in England by Sismondi, the fact that Say, to deny reality, had to dream up his cockeyed "law" in 1803, that the *Communist Manifesto* of 1848 was aware of the seriousness of crises, that Veblen spoke of depression as being normal and prosperity as being an occasional flash in the pan. It might also be argued that past depressions were not cured by an automatic restoration of equilibrium (whatever *that* is) but by governmental action and exogenous forces. Recovery from the depression of the 1870's may be traced in large part to bumper wheat and corn crops here accompanied by crop failures in Europe. But if we stop at every fireplug to check up on Galbraith, we shall never reach our proximate goal, which is to summarize the argument of his *Economics and the Public Purpose.*

His case is perhaps stronger concerning inflation, which, he says, also originates in the planning system and spills over into the market system. I, myself, prefer Paul Einzig's forthright statement that we have had 4,000 years of inflation. The advantage of this broad view is that inflation can be explained as a time-tested institution designed to impose upon the underlying population. But, after all, Galbraith is writing about the inflation of today, not the debasement of the coinage dolorously noted by Oresme or Bodin before 1600, or past surges of gold. His diagnosis and cure for the present are not markedly different from what has already been discussed on earlier pages. As the reader will remember, the Keynesian remedies will not do, and wage-price control in the planning system must be undertaken.

In the last chapter of this breather, Galbraith lists the faults of the economic system and the weakness of the remedies, if any, proposed by standard theory. The faults are: "unequal development, inequality, frivolous and erratic innovation, environmental assault, indifference to personality, power over the state, inflation, failure in inter-industry coordination."[6] If one views the economic world as standard theory views it, little can, or will, be done to cure these evils. But if one keeps in mind the Galbraithian model, changes and corrections are possible. And to this we now turn.

Before he launches himself and us on this unquiet sea, he issues a few warnings. First, reform begins not with laws and government but with how we view the economic system. Second, reform depends on recognition that things are not working. Third, attempts at reform may be hopeless but we shall never know unless we try. Next, he seeks to destroy confidence in hoary, but highly esteemed, proposals that simply do not work, such as antitrust, public regulation of utilities, and the like. Less ancient but equally feeble is to put representatives of the public, of consumers, of blacks, of women, of trade unions on the boards of mature corporations. The full-time pros of the technostructure will with ease, courtesy, and urbanity neutralize the influence of the part-time amateurs. Public ownership is not a general solution. A bureaucracy is a bureaucracy whether in or out of government. Neither the Atomic Energy Commission nor the Department of Defense puts the public purpose above its own. The symbiosis of the technostructure and the relevant governmental bureaucracy is apparently possible because they understand one another, like Brahmin calling to Brahmin.

So much for policies that will not work: now for reforms that stand a better chance of succeeding — proposals with moxie. Most important is emancipation of belief. The first item he mentions here is a change in the current pedagogy of economics. I assume this refers to the college level and would mean getting rid of Samuelson's textbook and its imitators. Standard economic theory perpetuates theories than can only give comfort to the planning system. This, of course, does not mean that the Samuelsons have dishonorably sold out to the leaders of the planning system. It only means that they are babes in the wood. One may agree with this reform, as I heartily do, yet believe that this is a most feeble remedy. Economic instruction as a formal thing comes when young people have already reached the age of about nineteen, and only to a fraction of those. But by then their minds are already so full of what the Augean Stables were also full of that it would require a Hercules and the river Alpheus to tidy things up. The conventional wisdom and the Protestant Ethic are absorbed with Gerber's baby food and then stamped solidly into the child's mind by radio, television, parents, playmates, and elementary-school teachers. Even the teaching of arithmetic helps to pound in the conventional wisdom:

Johnny has a paper route. He buys 50 papers for $6.00 and sells them for $7.50. What percentage profit does he make?

The books never pose a problem like this:

Count the number of girls in your grade and then the number who say they believe in the women's liberation movement. Do the same thing for the girls in the next higher grade. In which grade is the percentage of "women's libbers" greater?

A second similar and equally difficult way of emancipating belief is to attack the ingrained faith that high income is coordinate with social achievement. Our educational system perpetuates the belief that vocational training, including higher vocational training in science, law, business, is a central educational goal. Training in the creative arts is recreational, secondary, desirable but unimportant. Educators have a special responsibility to attack and uproot this attitude.

A third item in emancipation of belief is the building up of resistance to advertising and the allied arts. Whoever allows himself to be persuaded by advertising yields something of himself to the planning system. A blab-off on the TV set might help.

The fourth relates to the "manufacture of the public policy." Public policy originates in: the federal bureaucracy which is symbiotically related to the technostructure; in the work of the "literate acolytes" of the planning system, mostly lawyers; and in the universities. The universities do turn out dissenters and others attached to the public purpose, but in the teaching of economics and government, dissenters are few and those few get nowhere. Public policies originating from the sources listed just above are suspect and should be viewed as probably serving the needs of the planning system, not the public purpose.

From the emancipation of belief he goes on to discuss the emancipation of women. He puts forward the idea that women's liberation will enlarge and strengthen the service industries, which are a part of the market system, and this system should be strengthened. But is this true? External services are not always substitutes for labor in the house. Automatic washing and drying machines, powerful detergents, nonpuckering fabrics, the increasing popularity of casual clothes combine to displace the external laundry and old-fashioned washing in basement tubs or by the river. And much of what is used in this home process is produced by the planning system. Although TV dinners are now expensive and rated even below the messes mother used to make, nothing prevents their being improved and produced by the planning system. And, anyhow, the planning system is already degrading our palates. The day will come when we shall patriotically eat whatever it produces. This generation of Americans, for example, already prefers the dreadful, processed cheese of the planning system to the finer cheeses of the market system. For a *Feinschmecker* of this vintage nothing excels a tasteless hamburger on a degenerate roll and french fries drenched with catsup (from Del Monte, a member of the planning system).

From the emancipation of women we go on to the emancipation of the state. This is a most important chapter. The question at issue is how to reduce the power of the planning system over the state and increase the power of the market system. Galbraith's answer is the logical outcome of his view of the state — a view that none of us got through pretty Miss Eddingfield in the seventh grade, or even from Charles A. Beard in college. He develops with much sophistication the views he put forward in *Who Needs the Democrats?* The state can serve the public purpose or it can serve the planning system, and in recent decades it has tended to serve the latter primarily. The executive and his bureaucracy are now more powerful than the Congress. Congress formerly served special interests partly because its distinguished members were bribed by nineteenth-century entrepreneurs, and their twentieth-century holdovers. They could legally make goodwill contributions, but the modern corporation cannot. The executive was looked upon as the representative of all the people. He and his small bureaucracy could be looked upon as a countervailing force against a well-bribed Congress. But things have turned around. The symbiotic relationship between the governmental bureaucracy and the bureaucracy of the associated technostructure has brought them to see eye to eye on many matters and has superseded the old-fashioned system of buying up members of Congress. Thus the bureaucracies concerned with defense work hand in glove with the suppliers of weapons and military materials. To this general rule there are exceptions. The suppliers also have allies in the chairmen or members of the great committees, who are rewarded by having assigned to their districts airfields, bridges, roads, factories, and the like. This of course, helps reelection, and reelection preserves seniority. Thus, a few congressmen are still captives of the planning system: but Congress as a whole is less devoted to that system and is available to serve the market system and the public purpose.

The aim of the voter should be to fracture this pattern. The first available expedient is to stop electing incumbents. This, presumably, would prevent the cementing of warm relations between legislators and the bureaucracy and would shoot holes through the present maleficent seniority system. As for the president, if he is sensitive to the public purpose, he may now lead the Congress to exhibit equal sensitivity; if he is weak, a sensitive Congress may be able to sway the president. The key to the emancipation of the state is the Congress.

Assuming now that we have emancipated the state, what do we do next? Several lines of public action become possible and necessary to improve present economic arrangements and therefore the quality of life.

We must enhance the power of the market system and reduce the power of the planning system. This will bring about more nearly equal performance and income in the two systems. We are already doing some of the kinds of things he recommends. This is a really important point, for Galbraith seeks rather to press on with reforms that are already going on in fact than to introduce revolutionary solutions. He wants us to realize that "circumstances" are already compelling us to do sensible things even though they run counter to the conventional wisdom. I do not remember his defining the word "circumstance" anywhere, but I assume he means the uninhibited and unguided succession or drift of events. This could include such diverse things as the constant erosion of the soil, the increase of population, the multiplication of corpses on our highways, the unchecked swarming of live rats in the slums. It could also refer to the results of adhering to the doctrines of Adam Smith with obdurate tenacity of purpose despite the vast difference between our economy and that of 1776. When unexamined and habitual activities reach a point of crisis, we do something about them, regardless of religion, economic doctrines, sex, belief system, or marital state. Thus, in defiance of our most cherished beliefs, we have long strengthened the market system by agricultural price fixing, soil banks, and the like. We have made loans to small business despite Spencer's plea to let the weak perish for the common good; we have minimum-wage legislation despite the better instincts of the better people. During the great depression we had federal projects for painters, actors, and writers despite the widespread feeling that art is for homosexuals. Galbraith would support all such aids to the marketing system. In addition he would urge that small firms be allowed to form guilds without hindrance from antitrust. The trade unions of the market system should be encouraged, as they now are not; the discriminatory terms of the Wagner Act are still operative. And last, a guaranteed income should be provided those who do not find jobs in either the planning or market system. Galbraith appears not to be much worried about unemployment if this remedy becomes available. Indeed, he cares little about the "work ethic." The virtues of character building by work have been overrated.

Galbraith would have us reduce the incomes of the moguls within the planning system. Here he refers not only to the very large incomes themselves but also to the very generous and untaxed perquisites of the top corporation brass, from private toilets and bars to executive dining rooms and stock options and, in earlier days, spittoons in imitation of the work of Benvenuto Cellini. Without casting wholesale doubt on the distributive theory of marginal productivity (as Clarence E. Ayres did), Galbraith believes the theory has no validity here. Here power determines all, or nearly all — something that puts him in agreement with Bertrand de Jouvenal.[7] He goes on to make the interesting observation that the traditional role of women helps to perpetuate great differences of income, since women are assigned to much of the lower-grade white-collar work, and nobody dreams of promoting them to any post much higher than that of straw boss of the typing pool.

Progressive income taxation should play a part in the task of income equalization,[8] but huge incomes themselves should be pared down in the first instance. To award a man a huge income, even if much of it is taxed away is to perpetuate the myth that it was earned. Since the income was obtained by the exercise of power, it was not really earned, and the fiction of enormous productivity by high corporation officials must not be supported. He further suggests that the fully mature corporation, which he describes as the firms that have "fully completed the euthanasia of stockholder power" should be transformed into a fully public corporation.[9] The company's stock would be traded in for government securities paying fixed interest. This policy would do away with adventitious gains.

Galbraith then proceeds to the question of nationalizing some industries. He realizes that this proposal brings us face to face with the unacceptable word "socialism." He seeks to exorcise the evil spirit residing in the word by calling attention to the fact that circumstances have already brought us to the brink of socialism in two areas. One is the area of unsatisfactory performance in both the market system and the planning system. We perform unsatisfactorily in housing, medical service, and public transport. In all three industries government steps in to give aid in all sorts of bewildering and eccentric ways. In all three we already have something close to socialism, but very poor socialism. "The only answer for these industries," he writes, "is full organization under public ownership. This is the new socialism which searches not for the positions of power in the economy but for the positions of weakness."[10]

As for the other area in which the new socialism should be inaugurated, it is paradoxically at the other extreme: where the planning system is too strong. Galbraith had already pointed out in an article in the *New York Times Magazine* of November 16, 1969, that the large defense firms should be nationalized since they are already virtually socialized except in name. Now, let's go all the way, he says.

Before leaving Galbraith's "new socialism" we should note that his socialism is not ideological; it is the result again of circumstances. His reforms do not flow out of the labor theory of value or dialectical materialism or the doctrine of class struggle. These lead to Utopianism. His do not rest on the belief in the perfectibility of mankind. They are, rather, pragmatic reforms based on current circumstances, or the unchecked drift of events.

We come next to the environment. As everybody knows, both producer and consumer are guilty of defacing, polluting, poisoning, injuring, and eviscerating the environment. And as everybody knows, absolutism in this area has its penalities; the costs of protection may be greater than the costs of reasonable environmental deterioration. A little carbon monoxide is preferable to the return of the non-polluting sedan chair.

For environmental control, the legislature, not the bureaucracies, should take over, assisted by a competent technical staff. The relevant bureaucracies of government, in symbiotic relationship with the technostructures of business, lack the will to serve the public purpose.

It is a cardinal principle of Galbraith that congressmen hearken to the public purpose and that the president (with his bevy of bureaucracies) does not. There are exceptions, of course; some of the senior and more powerful legislators are extensions of the bureaucracies and therefore of the planning system. Until a better balance between the market system and the planning system than we now have can be achieved, the legislature should systematically seek to reduce the power of the planning system. This can be done in part through the effect of money appropriated (or not) for various projects; for example, the supersonic transport was killed by withholding funds. The job should be done by a well-staffed congressional committee. When the national budget is agreed upon, the congress must stay within the limits prescribed.

We come next to the issue of stabilizing the economy. Here Galbraith has four basic proposals. First, both corporation and personal income taxes should be made sharply progressive. Over the years we have lost sight of this goal, and serious loopholes have been admitted into the system. This trend should be reversed. Second, governmental expenditure should emphasize spending for public purposes rather than for armaments or exploring the moon, Mars, and Venus. The amount to be raised by taxation is determined by the need for public services. Spending should be channeled into the hands of people who do not save much of their income — that is, to people of low income. Third, reliance on monetary policy should be minimized. Fourth, against inflation, wage-price control should be effective and permanent in the planning system. Unlike several other economists who are now asking whether inflation really hurts anybody, Galbraith has not budged. Inflation is against the public purpose.

We come at long last to the final chapters in which Galbraith touches on the need for interindustry planning. This has little to do with the planning system — something that may confuse the hurried reader. Some sort of overall planning authority will have to issue an early warning if not enough electricity is being produced to keep up with all the appliances being sold by the appliance industry. And, of course, this procedure goes for all other mismatched production. He does not go into much detail.

What may be a little surprising to most readers is that to Galbraith our foreign trade difficulties are analogous to our unsolved planning problems at home. Aggregate American capital is badly distributed among industries. Too much goes for the armaments industries and too little for consumers' products. Thus Japan and Germany are ahead of us, along with a few unspecified nations, and we overbuy from them. Our inflation does not help matters.

Standard theory, foreseeing such imbalances, long ago developed theories about how, under free trade, competition, peace, and other unrealistic conditions, such disequilibria would automatically bring equilibrating forces into play. But Galbraith considers such theories hogwash, or, to use the language of the polished gentleman that he is, they are "partly fraudulent, partly incompetent and for the rest, extensively irrelevant."[11] The monetary experts hold their conferences and banquets, discuss nonsense, paper over a crisis, and come back home to await a new crisis. The only remedy based on reality is to coordinate the planning policies of the several national planning systems: "This must include common policies in the distribution of capital as between industries, common steps to control the wage-price spiral."[12] But this solution is beyond the ability of any international agency and, of course, cannot be done unilaterally. Improvement, however, is not hopeless. If the United States planned its economy better and clarified its policies abroad, the other nations would have to adapt their policies to ours, as they did in the years following the Second World War, when currency crises and the like occurred less frequently. All of this is said with a compression that taxes the reader.

The book ends with a plea to economists to open up their minds to the role of power in economic life.

The book appeared so recently that, at this writing, only a few reviews have appeared, and most of them have been published in news dailies or weeklies. Those I have seen have been competent enough, but they come nearer to news reporting than to thoughtful evaluation. Reviews by economists in the scholarly quarterlies will probably not appear until 1974. Galbraith will be flayed alive for his sinful heterodoxy and commended for his wit, elegance of language, and so on. The latter will please him as it pleases a beautiful and intelligent woman to be told she is beautiful. But both Galbraith and the beauty can get rather bored at ceaseless and unoriginal praise. Both long to be praised for other reasons. Galbraith would, I think, like to be told that his model of the economy — even with its imperfections — is closer to reality than that of standard theory. And this praise he will not get from the scholarly journals.

CHAPTER 8

Evaluation

THE time has come to evaluate our subject. He is versatile, serious, witty, intelligent, philosophic — a man of action as well as thought. His fame reaches across several continents and social classes. Obviously, economists and governmental officials know him, but he is also widely known among all cultivated groups and all professions from teachers to lawyers, clergymen, and proctologists. One cannot doubt that Galbraith is an extraordinary man. Some of his admirers might be tempted to call him a Renaissance man, but that, I think, is going too far.

Acquaintances, knowing I was doing this book, have sent me helpful clippings from many places here and in Europe, informing me that Galbraith had written this or done that, including one news photo from a village in Maine showing him about to take off in the kilt to do figure skating for a Boston charity. Not all were sent in a friendly mood: the figure-skating picture was accompanied by an aspersive comment about Galbraith's vanity and his desire to show off his "damn' legs below the kilt" and a clipping from Aiguebellette commenting: "How did he build up such a smooth publicity machine?" I am sure he has no such machine, but I am also sure that he avoids keeping candles under bushels. But the point I am making is that everybody knows the man and his activities are noted by the press almost everywhere.

Economists, in judging him, divide into two major groups: standard economists and heretics or near-heretics. I have already, in earlier chapters, intimated that standard economists, often professing to admire his graceful language, his wit, his general intelligence, versatility, deplore his economic theory; he disregards the work of others, or echoes old or presumably discarded ideas; he tears down without building up; he is full of value statements — something that marks a man as being totally devoid of the scientific spirit. A winner of the Nobel Prize for the dismal science is said to have described Galbraith as "the non-economist's economist." Most of this and other contumely is quite sincere, at least on the level of conscious thought. Actually, in the depths of the unconscious the critics probably realize that if they adopted the Galbraithian brand of economics they would be threatened as silent film stars were threatened in the late 1920's when sound came in. Standard economists, most of them, have not yet made contact with heterodoxy, and they would be in a rather bad way if the heterodox became orthodox. Since they have a strong instinct for survival, as Galbraith has noted, they must repudiate the unfamiliar vigorously.

It may be observed in passing that the heterodox economist must, to stay afloat academically, be as proficient in standard theory as a run-of-the-mill orthodox economist. The standard economist need know nothing about heterodoxy, except perhaps a little smattering of Marx. This is to say that a dissenter is a more completely educated man, having made wider studies in philosophy, anthropology, history, psychology, and sociology than the orthodox economist. It is my belief, unproved as yet, that unless one is to the manner born, one must go through a profoundly emotional experience, like a religious conversion or deconversion to become a dissenter. The problem is that of resistance: turning away from what is unpleasant. Standard theorists have so closely identified themselves with one view of the economic world that it causes torment to reject it. This view does not arise from formal instruction alone; instruction in the moral values of the competitive, money-using economy and in the Protestant Ethic begins before nursery school. This includes the apologetics and immoral concepts of our economic system of thought and to give these up is painful, lèse majesté, and sacrilegious. Thus the standard economist does all he can to avoid seeing the economic world with clear gaze and avoids reading Galbraith sympathetically. Galbraith will never get high grades from orthodox colleagues. They will — as has been said — dwell kindly on his wit, style, irony, height, and royalties to show that their unfriendly criticism is not a personal matter. As a matter of fact, Galbraith's economics would probably be all but neglected by the high cockalora of the profession if Galbraith had not first won acclaim as a luminous bureaucrat, gifted writer, and Harvard professor.

A word about the Marxists and Galbraith at this point. They applaud his heterodoxy, but when all is said and done they feel that he is merely a supporter of monopoly capitalism — a sophisticated one, and for that reason all the more dangerous to Marxism. Galbraith downgrades the force of the class struggle and of the working classes, slurs over the evils of imperialism, and overlooks the power and ruthlessness of the ruling classes if attacked. The likelihood that Galbraith's scientific and educational estate can develop a countervailing power can only be entertained by a naive mind. In sum, Galbraith turns out to be in their opinion, a flaccid but clever liberal.[1]

The heterodox economists obviously have much more sympathy for, and understanding of, Galbraith than the orthodox do. He is one of them and deserves any reasonable break. Nonetheless, there are some reservations, some ambivalence, an occasional dash of ignorance, and perhaps a shade of jealousy. In 1973 I sent out a questionnaire concerning Galbraith to some forty members of the Association for Evolutionary Economics. Though the Association gladly accepts the dues of almost anybody, it is likely that here we have a concentration of American heterodox economists (there are some Europeans). Some of the questions were structured (answer "yes" or "no"; arrange in order, etc.) while others solicited comments. Let me first quote some of the solicited comments. Each observation is by a different person:

Unlike Veblen he is not a major seminal thinker. I only wish I could have rated Kenneth with Myrdal, but I can't feel that he battled as humbly as Myrdal, and humility is my test of greatness.

Is sometimes careless with selection and interpretation of evidence. Useful fellow to have around but the net result will be small.

Extremely effective, useful, important; basically unoriginal yet extremely influential.

Deep thinker who could have been a major system builder.

Popularizer.

Galbraith . . . is probably much smarter and knowledgeable about the defects of the present economic and social order than he indicates . . . through his writings. I do not admire this trait and have always attributed it to his membership in what is now popularly called the establishment.

His originality is not confined to economics.

He is original as a social critic, not as an economist.

Veblen requires rewriting in the idiom of each period. Hence it is no disgrace [that Galbraith should] use Veblen as a model.

One of the leading American institutionalists and an authority on Veblen used both the structured and unstructured parts of the questionnaire to say several times that almost every important idea of Galbraith's may be found in Veblen, yet he checked a box labeled "original thinker" — something that seems a little inconsistent. It must, however, be stated that questionnaires can be confusing to all concerned.

Below I reproduce part of the actual questionnaire and insert the number of checks marked by members of the Association of Evolutionary Economics.

1. Of the four well-known economists listed below, how would you evaluate their contribution to the development of economic thought? Check appropriate spaces (4 checks).

	Very great	Great	Moderate	Negligible
Friedman	1	6	8	6
Galbraith	4	13	6	—
Myrdal	6	9	3	—
Samuelson	5	7	8	2

2. I have, in speaking to economists and others, heard all of the following words or phrases seriously used to describe Galbraith. Which do you think are most appropriate? Add one or two of your own on the space provided if you think the ones given do not fit. Do not check or write in more than three items.

0	Scientific	6	Honest
1	Smart Aleck	3	Lacking in rigor
12	Needed iconoclast	3	Egocentric
3	Mere imitator of Veblen	6	Good scholar
1	Superficial	4	Courageous
4	Profound	11	Original thinker
1	Just a journalist	1	Just a phrase maker
		13	Brilliant social critic

It is strange that a group like this, mostly heterodox, should give Samuelson more "very greats" than Galbraith. On the other hand if the "greats" and "very greats" are added together, Galbraith scores 17 and Samuelson 12. Also, nobody considered Galbraith to be "negligible," while two placed the Nobel prize winner in that category. One must not disengage hard and fast conclusions from the above. The sample was small and the sampling error must be astronomical. Joan Robinson, who, I regret, did not receive a questionnaire, has written in another connection that Gunnar Myrdal, of all living economists, "has made the most important contributions to the subject."[2] Thus, an authoritative voice and, I am sure a sympathetic one, has placed Galbraith below Mydral.

This report does not exhaust the questionnaire. I learned further that almost all responders were teachers of economics and that almost all required their students to read at least one book of Galbraith's. The books fall into the following order of frequency: *New Industrial State, American Capitalism, Affluent Society*. One might deduce that Galbraith is well-known in colleges — as is Samuelson, whose textbook is to be found all over the place. The questionnaire shows considerable admiration for Galbraith, but also some want of esteem and, surprisingly for members of such an organization, an astonishing respect for Samuelson. If the sample is trustworthy, the explanation may lie in the fact that Samuelson's policies are moderately liberal, whatever may be said of his theories, and some liberal economists may think of themselves and of him as heterodox. And anyhow, I emphasize again, not all members of the AFEE are heterodox. To be a heterodox economist one must, I think, repudiate the basic model of Adam Smith, even if — as in the case of Samuelson — that model is hedged by amendments, reservations, backpedaling, and prodigal use of *einerseits* and *anderseits*.

To summarize, orthodox theorists repudiate Galbraith as an economist, though they may admire him as a satirist, liberal, politician, bureaucrat, writer, and gifted bread winner. They may even half agree with some of his ideas and proposed reforms. And of course, everybody likes to believe himself to be in favor of improving the quality of life. Heterodox economists, on the other hand, are happy that a strong, eloquent voice is carrying on and continuing the long and honorable tradition of dissent. They are not wholly pleased with him, however. He is not quite the heterodox economists' heterodox economist.

Perhaps Allan Gruchy's opinion of Galbraith is one of the best informed. Gruchy is a reliable heterodox economist and much of his writing has handled the problem of dissent. He feels that national programming is the next step in the development of heterodox theory. He has great admiration for the recusants of previous generations (Veblen, Mitchell, Commons, Tugwell, J. M. Clark, G. Means) but regrets that they were hampered by the fact that certain tools had not yet been developed in their day.[3] Since then, says Gruchy, systems analysis, operations research, computerized econometric models, linear programming, and so on, have been developed. Even Clarence Ayres and Gunnar Myrdal — men of a later vintage — have not availed themselves of the tools, and Galbraith, still younger, has not seen their usefulness. The late Gerhard Colm had, however, joined the old heterodoxy with the new tools. He was, to Gruchy, the very pattern of a modern major 'conomist. Galbraith's lack of interest in planning or national programming is for Gruchy the source of his failure to scale the peaks. I have just received a letter from Gruchy. After reading Galbraith's *Economics and the Public Purpose,* he acknowledges that Galbraith has partly corrected this deficiency in his latest book.

How sound is this criticism? National programs are at present likely to fall on barren ground in the United States. There is no use planning what cannot be, at least in the calculable future. The conventional wisdom must first be the object of considerable erosion. Western Europe is more receptive to the idea of indicative planning and national programming than the United States. We still cling desperately to the myths of individual initiative, *laissez-faire,* and private enterprise, and we do not tolerate the idea of planning (despite the fact that much planning does go on). Our federal government, with its tradition of state's rights, makes us balk at national economic legislation. We are perhaps too much of a warfare state to plan far ahead, since we are constantly at the mercy of unexpected events generated by others.[4] Western Europe has done much better than we have about keeping the peace since 1946. The presidential system as opposed to the parliamentary system is cumbersome. Our vast size and motley regions with their differing needs make planning difficult.

Europeans are, no doubt, much better off now than they were in 1946, in motors of all kinds, telephones, roads, hydrogen bombs, TV sets, cola drinks, plastic packaging, and so on. This growth may be attributed in part to national programming, but ordinary economic development and technological progress would have accounted for much of it anyhow. The quality of life, apart from benefits conferred by advances in medical science, has probably not improved much in Western Europe. Homicide by automobile is catching on all over. The voice of the snowmobile, one can safely predict, will soon be heard from Haute Savoie to the Bernese Oberland. It is not clear that Western Europe has made adequate plans to meet the petroleum shortage of the winter of 1973-74. Roman traffic cops have to take a fix of oxygen every hour or so. Naples is invaded by the plague. The Via Veneto is befouled by the blue smoke of automobiles; the splashing fountains of the lovely piazzas cannot be heard above the decibel-laden air of the Seven Hills. Europeans seem to enjoy polluting land, sea, and air as much as we Americans do. High-rise hotels are invading the ski resorts. In Paris at least, if not in the provinces, the good, little, out-of-the-way restaurants famed of yore, are giving way to spic-and-span self-service counters with all of the gastronomical distinction of diners in Utica, New York.[5] I do not, of course, deny that great restaurants still exist in Paris. To summarize, the quality of life in Western Europe has not improved much under indicative planning. It is doubtful whether Galbraith and Colm are very far apart in their ultimate goals. Colm deplores the fact that not enough of our resources go into public goods and speaks of the mediocre "quality of life in an age of quantitative material abundance."[6] This comment is very Galbraithian. I would be inclined to say that both Colm and Galbraith are needed if we are to improve the quality of life and realize the other benefits of a well-ordered economy. Before the seed of a Colm can sprout, however, the stony ground must be prepared by a Galbraith. Until important segments of our society can see how inadequately we are faring, how ridiculously chained we are to a dead past, we shall never be willing to accept national planning, or indicative planning, or anything else that serves the public purpose generously. It is the job of the Galbraiths to use their economic knowledge and their gifts of persuasion and satire to make us see how badly off we really are. The great satirists of modern times have had the public purpose in view — Anatole France, G. B. Shaw, George Orwell, and all the rest, major and minor. Their function is to make us want something better and this Galbraith is doing. His role is as important as Colm's, but it is a different one.

One parting shot. Colm's work reminds me of some of Leonardo da Vinci's drawings. On paper Leonardo da Vinci drew serviceable flying machines and other excellent engines. But they were mostly useless because no lightweight source of power had yet come into existence. And so his designs for helicopters, for example, were sterile. Colm's plans must be powered by a public will which does not yet exist. Whether Galbraith can cause such a public will to crystallize is an open question. He himself has doubts. I, too, have doubts. It seems to me that by this time he ought to be the center of a Galbraithian school of young followers if his influence is to spread far and securely in this century. To the best of my knowledge there is no such school, or group. The Association for Evolutionary Economics does not cluster around him, though it would, I think, if he made an effort. It is the obvious group for him to use. No swarms of Ph.D. candidates hover around him, I am told. It is true that he is a big wheel in the liberal wing of the Democratic party, and that his speeches and advice are sought by the Stevensons, Kennedys, and McGoverns of the party. That's fine, but such men seem to have a genius for losing.

I share with my colleagues, both orthodox and unorthodox, some annoyance with Galbraith's "audacious charlatanism," a phrase used about Veblen by Eric Roll. Several times, in the preceding pages, I have stopped to question the breadth or truth of some of Galbraith's vast generalizations. He does say astonishing things sometimes. If he were as careful of his facts as of his prose, he would inspire greater confidence. A contemporary poet — perhaps Auden — has said that the job of the poet is "to defend the language." Galbraith seems to want to share this job. Excellent, but one sometimes wishes that Galbraith, with his impeccable sentences and his peccable facts, would spend more time on the latter than on the former.

Despite his obvious scholarship, his well-stocked mind, and his sagacious insights, one is struck by a parallel to the ironic observation of one of the Scandinavians that Keynes was "unnecessarily original." Surely this could also be said of Galbraith. When he discusses a subject he takes off violently and rides fiercely into the dawn of a new day as if nobody had ever taken that direction before. But, like Keynes, he is not so original as all that. He has plenty of footnotes on current writers, going all the way back to Gardiner Means and A. A. Berle, but the chariness of his footnotes referring to Veblen, John Dewey, J. M. Clark, J. A. Hobson, Clarence Ayres,

Myrdal, Joan Robinson, R. G. Tugwell, and Wesley Mitchell, is indeed striking. It may be more interesting than important to note that in his recent *China Passage* he makes no mention of Joan Robinson's *Cultural Revolution in China.*[6] The two economists have much in common and, of course, they are personally acquainted. He has a moral obligation to let us know that he belongs to a tradition, not to write as if he were founding one. All would benefit by his being a team player. Although much of his work is, in a sense, based on anthropology, he reveals little interest in what anthropology has to say to economists. I asked him once if he had read much of Dewey or John A. Hobson. He said no. By denying Dewey he denied a philosopher who was as important to heterodox economics as Bentham was to orthodox; by denying Hobson, he denied not only an important quality-of-life economist, but also John Ruskin, who, like Dewey, provided underpinnings for economic dissent. Ruskin deeply influenced economics at Oxford and created the climate for Toynbee, Tawney, and Hobson — and, indeed, for all who revolted against what Ruskin called "the huxter science."[7] Art — as everybody knows — was at least as important to Ruskin as it is to Galbraith.

For reasons which I cannot defend, I have long thought of Galbraith as the potential John Dewey of economics — the Dewey particularly of the *Reconstruction of Philosophy.* In outward things the men are completely different. I used to see Dewey walk into Teachers College at Columbia looking slightly bewildered and countrified, carrying a couple of crates of eggs from his farm for delivery to customers on the faculty. I have not seen Galbraith often, but when I do see him in person or in pictures, he is always well dressed and urbane. Dewey's writing was awkward; Galbraith's prose flows like the body of a gifted ballet dancer. Galbraith makes his vanity bearable by the humorous device of exaggerating it; if Dewey exaggerated anything, it was his humility.

But now for the similarities. Both have been active in reform politics. Both saw that their fields of study — philosophy and economics, respectively — have not really been a search for truth, but rather a search for myths to explain this curious and unreasonable world: such things as high and low rank, abject poverty and ridiculously great wealth, domination and obedience.[8] Both saw that these myths, though perhaps once serviceable to mankind, are no longer relevant. Dewey invented instrumentalism as a guiding philosophy and Galbraith is (seemingly) an unconscious instrumentalist who, like Molière's M. Jourdain, had unwittingly been speaking prose for forty years. Even though Galbraith does not have the singleness of purpose that characterized Dewey, he has done pretty well with his left hand — and this is perhaps the tragedy of Galbraith — not for himself, for he seems to be having a good time living out his life in his own way. But for the rest of us it is too bad.

Appraising Galbraith's place in history is, at this time, a rather bootless endeavor, except to suggest that he may indeed have a place in history. First of all, as a white male between 65 - 70, he has 13.2 years left to live, but being now reasonably healthy and of moderate habits, he may have still more time in which to exert an even greater influence than he does today. Second, history is capricious and to use Galbraith's phrase, "The moving finger sticks." Columbus, not Leif Ericson, is recognized as the discoverer of America; Robert Fulton is hailed as the inventor of the steamboat, while poor John Fitch slunk off to commit suicide somewhere in Kentucky. François Quesnay rather than Smith has a strong claim to the title of "father of economics." Thus, we must consider that, even if Galbraith richly deserves to be remembered across the centuries, fate may yet turn him into something no bigger than a footnote.

But does he richly deserve? Here, again, only the turn of events can give us an answer. Smith and Marx have become famous and their names have endured by a sort of posthumous charisma. A large fraction of mankind has, in each case, accepted the grand designs of the two men and posterity has molded a large part of the world into the images — more or less — that they first created.

Galbraith has also given us a grand design — a new model, especially with his most recent book. The model is that of a world divided into two economic systems: the planning system and the market system. The dynamics of each is different, partly because one is strong and one is weak, and partly because technology favors one and not the other. The first often overrides the public purpose; the other comes closer to serving the public purpose. The stronger system is powerful enough to shape some of the uglier aspects of our culture. The state — perhaps like the Sabine women — is waiting to see who its captor will be. It now yields to the stronger planning system but is not averse to abduction by the market system, if that can be arranged. If unchecked, the planning system will attack the quality of life until little life or quality is left. But the educational and scientific estate — an inevitable by-product of the planning system —

may, with allies, capture the state. Its allies are the market system and such organized liberals as may be found in the left wing of the Democratic Party. To do this the educational and scientific estate must, in this country, capture the Congress. The bureaucracies of the executive branch are too closely tied up with the bureaucracies of the planning system to initiate changes that would improve the quality of life. They are not worth capturing, though they should be sheared of power. Once the state is in safe hands we must proceed with reform: wage-price fixing in the planning system, making incomes more nearly equal, introducing governmental ownership in certain areas, and the like. This plan is not Utopian; Galbraith does not promise a rose garden — just something better.

I have, of course, set forth only an abstraction of an abstraction, but I do not think I have misrepresented the Galbraithian model. Now, the point is that, if enough people accept this model and this analysis, Galbraith will turn out to be a great economist and history will find a large place for him in its pantheon. He cannot force this acceptance alone. Like Smith, Marx, Darwin, and Freud, he must have his Epigoni.

Some will say that the model does not accord with reality and that the analysis is defective. That objection, of course, if true, would be a hindrance but not a fatal one. The models of Marx, Smith, Freud, and Darwin were faulty. The current model of standard economic theory is an anachronism, yet thousands of poor undergraduates accept it every year. The real question is not whether Galbraith's grand design conforms to reality, but whether it has the possibility of being widely accepted. I for one think it has. And the reason I think it has is that the model, whatever its defects, comes closer to reality than the models of standard theory and of Marx.

But perhaps we are up a little too high in the ionosphere. Let's get back to a more sober consideration of Galbraith's calculable influence. There is a degree of influence to which he may reasonably aspire: influencing the minds of many young and capable economists, encouraging them to be big thinkers instead of little thinkers, and introducing the concepts of power and public purpose as central topics of economic discourse.

In summary, then, what Galbraith is trying to get us to do is to make us see the world as it is today, not as it appears through lenses first fitted to our eyes two hundred years ago and slightly modified a long generation ago. Last winter I stayed in Southern California with a painter friend of mine. As he painted the ocean, rocks, and sky, the natives would come up to admire, ask questions, or offer criticism. Once, when the sky was a sort of leaden rose, and my friend had painted it that way, one of the aborigines said, "I like your picture, mister, but shouldn't the sky be blue?" Long experience had given my friend patience in these matters, and he replied quietly, "Perhaps you're right; next time, maybe." I'm afraid that many economists are like the indigene. He thinks the sky should be painted blue because in nursery school he was told the sky is blue and later he learned some sentimental lines about the sky is blue and I love you, or my blue heaven; in high school he was taught about the patch of blue that prisoners call the sky and about the Air Force's wild blue yonder. But the sky is not always blue. I think what Galbraith is trying to do is to make us take a second look — this time a clear look at reality, not as it is conceived in that mixture of poetry, myth, and self-deception which is so much part of standard economic theory. And I hope and believe that in this he is succeeding.

Notes and References

Preface
*Clifton, New Jersey: Kelley, 1972.

Chapter 1
1. A woman of my acquaintance, who went to school with him in those days tells me that he was known as Kenneth, not Ken, and also as "Soupy."
2. *Who Needs the Democrats* (New York: New American Library, 1970), p. 9.
3. *Ambassador's Journal* (New York: New American Library, 1970), p. 335, footnote.
4. June, 1968, Vol. 5, no. 6.

Chapter Two
1. As the experienced social scientist will know, to have been influenced by Marx is not necessarily to be a Communist. Marx himself would probably be shocked at what has been done in his name since 1917. Entirely apart from his support for the expropriation of the rich, he made interesting and useful social, economic, and historical analyses. As in the case of Freud, whose ideas are widely accepted by non-Freudians, Marx has contributed insights that are accepted but not acknowledged by his enemies. Though Galbraith has explicitly avowed a debt to Marx, he has also explicitly disavowed Marxism as the basis of a program for political action.
2. Veblen was a true evolutionist. Marx wrote the *Manifesto* before the *Origin of Species* appeared and was nurtured in Hegelianism — a system of metaphysics that also found a place for institutional change; though the distinction between the two kinds of change may have some importance, it need not concern us here.
3. *The Instinct of Workmanship* (New York: Huebsch, 1922), p. 25.
4. This phrase is reprinted in his *Economics, Peace and Laughter* (Boston: Houghton Mifflin, 1971), p. 350.
5. As he does in two pamphlets: *Who Needs the Democrats* (New York: Doubleday, 1970 and New American Library, Inc., 1970) and *How to Control the Military* (New York: Doubleday, 1969). In both of these, like the

two Billy's (Sunday and Graham), his tone has the eloquence and unconvincing quality of the evangelist.

6. It is generally known that instincts have a dubious existence in modern psychology; I use the term partly because Veblen used it and partly because any other word is just as bad.

7. See my *Beyond Supply and Demand* (New York: Columbia University Press, 1946), *passim*.

8. See his *Modern Economic Thought* (New York: Prentice-Hall, 1947). pp. viii ff., and elsewhere in the same book.

Chapter Three

1. *Quarterly Journal of Economics* (May, 1936), pp. 456 - 75.

2. *American Economic Review* (June, 1936), pp. 235 - 47.

3. It appeared in *Review of Economics and Statistics* (May, 1941), pp. 82 - 85.

4. *Quarterly Journal of Economics* (August, 1946), pp. 475 - 89.

5. *American Economic Review* (June, 1947), pp. 287 - 302.

6. Dec., 1952, pp. 986 ff.

7. *American Capitalism,* p. 190.

8. Introduction to the Sentry edition (a reissue of the original) of *The Great Crash, 1929* (Boston: Houghton Mifflin, 1961) p. xix.

9. *General Theory* (New York: Harcourt, Brace, 1936), p. 159.

10. N.Y.: Charles Boni Paper Books, 1929. Stuart Chase got his basic materials from the Lynds' *Middletown* and from *Recent Economic Changes,* a study directed by Wesley Mitchell.

11. Paul H. Douglas, *Controlling Depression* (New York: W.W. Norton 1935).

12. This part of the story appears in another book by Galbraith entitled *Economics, Peace and Laughter,* p. 320.

13. *Ambassador's Journal,* p. 52, Signet edition. The niece was, of course, Elizabeth II.

Chapter Four

1. First published in Boston by Houghton Mifflin, 1958. All page references in this chapter are to the Mentor edition, New American Library, 1962.

2. *The Affluent Society,* p. 129.

3. See Samuelson's article "Economists and the History of Ideas," *American Economic Review,* LII, no. i (March 1962), 7. His subtopic at this point is *The Affluent Society.* In one of those playful passages that mar his work, Samuelson seems to be quoting a lot of unidentified economists who have found fault with *The Affluent Society.* One of them, evidently, had used Bentham's phrase, with which Samuelson presumably agrees, against Galbraith.

4. Gross neglect of the testimony of the other sciences would, of course,

invite censure. To argue for a restoration of the old Lambeth workhouse as a method of handling pauperism cheaply would not attract much applause, despite its economic soundness.

5. *The Affluent Society,* p. 205.

6. *Work and Wealth, A Human Valuation* (London: Allen and Unwin, 1914), pp. 43 ff.

Chapter Five

1. Adapted from the Lépine-de Douhet article in *Le Nouvel Observateur,* Paris, second trimester, 1971, p. 81.

2. *N.Y. Times,* Aug. 25, 1971, p. 33.

3. *New Industrial State,* rev. ed., p. 300.

4. Reprinted in his *Essays in Persuasion* (New York: Harcourt, Brace, 1932), pp. 358 ff.

5. *The New Industrial State,* rev. ed., p. 81.

6. *The Public Interest,* No. 9, Fall, 1967, p. 104.

7. These are closely related ideas, the first used in *The Affluent Society,* the second in *The New Industrial State.* Oddly enough, in my opinion at least, he never speaks of "The Dependence Effect" in the later book, though "The Revised Sequence" is almost the same thing.

8. *Southern Economic Journal,* 27 (April, 1961) 346.

9. March, 1959, pp. 112 ff. Author not mentioned.

10. In the book *Indian Painting* (Boston: Houghton-Mifflin, 1968), of which Galbraith is coauthor, this sad story appears. I wonder whether even Veblen conceived of conspicious consumption so imaginatively. Somewhere I have read of Cleopatra's dissolving pearls in vinegar and quaffing the brew; but that was just to show off; it is not reported that the draft caused even gastric rumblings under the surface of that lovely body.

11. See W.C. Mitchell, *Types of Economic Theory* (New York: Kelley, 1967), I, 321 ff.

12. Special issue, second quarter, 1971.

Chapter Six

1. Boston: Houghton-Mifflin, 1962.

2. This statement, of course, made more sense in 1962, when it was written.

3. There really are other exceptions; he quite obviously admires A. Harrimann, C. Bowles, and many others. Somewhere in his writing he pats "Tommy" on the back, whom I identify as the late Llewellyn Thompson, formerly ambassador to Russia.

4. Boston: Houghton Mifflin, 1968. I have to thank my friend Edward H. Dwight, of the Munson-Williams-Proctor Institute of Utica, for helping me to evaluate this book.

5. May 4, 1968.

Chapter Seven

1. *Provincial Letters*, XVI.
2. Boston: Houghton Mifflin, 1973.
3. *Economics and the Public Purpose,* p. 155.
4. *Ibid.* p. 172.
5. *N.Y. Times,* Sept. 2, 1973, section 3, p. 12.
6. *Op. cit.,* p. 211.
7. "Intellectuals and Power," *The Center Magazine,* VI, no. 1 (Jan.-Feb. 1973) 54.
8. Though Galbraith often uses "equal" (and its derivatives) without qualification, I am sure he means "more nearly equal."
9. *Op. cit.* p. 272.
10. *Ibid.* p. 279.
11. *Ibid.* p. 320.
12. *Ibid.* p. 322.

Chapter Eight

1. For an excellent and learned statement of the Marxist position on Galbraith, see Paul Sweezy's "Galbraith's Utopia," in the *N.Y. Review of Books* 20, no. 18 (Nov. 15, 1973), 3 ff.
2. *N.Y. Times Book Review,* Sept. 23, 1973, p. 31.
3. Allan, Gruchy. *Contemporary Economic Thought* (Clifton, N.J.: Augustus Kelley, 1972), Ch. 4.
4. These lines are being written in the first week of the Yom-Kippur war of 1973. This action involves us already in heavy unplanned expenses for the rearming of Israel. More than two billion dollars have just been asked for.
5. Compare with Georges Simenon's supporting evidence in his *Maigret and the Lazy Burglar* (New York: Harcourt Brace Jevanovich, Inc., 1973), p. 249.
6. Quoted by Gruchy, *op. cit.* p. 242.
7. London: Pelican Books, 1969.
8. See Paul T. Homan, *Contemporary Economic Thought* (New York: Harper, 1928), p. 290.
9. See B. Malinowski, "Myths and Origin" in *Magic, Science and Religion* (Garden City, N.Y.: Doubleday Anchor, 1954), pp. 111 ff.

Selected Bibliography

PRIMARY SOURCES

The following list names the books written by Galbraith. Each listing identifies the first hardcover edition, unless otherwise noted. Several of the books are now easily available in paperback format, mostly in the editions of the New American Library (now, in 1973, at Bergenfield, N.J.). The order is chronological.

Modern Competition and Business Policy. With H. S. Dennison. New York: Oxford University Press, 1938.

American Capitalism: The Concept of Countervailing Power. Cambridge, Mass.: Riverside Press, 1952.

A Theory of Price Control. Cambridge, Mass.: Harvard University Press, 1952.

Economics and the Art of Controversy. New Brunswick: Rutgers University Press, 1955.

The Great Crash, 1929. Boston: Houghton Mifflin, 1955.

The Affluent Society. Boston: Houghton Mifflin, 1958.

The Liberal Hour. Boston: Houghton Mifflin, 1960.

Economic Development in Perspective. Cambridge, Mass.: Harvard University Press, 1962.

The McLandress Dimension. Boston: Houghton Mifflin, 1962.

The Scotch. Cambridge, Mass.: Riverside Press, 1964.

Economic Development. Cambridge, Mass.: Harvard University Press, 1964.

The New Industrial State. Boston: Houghton Mifflin, 1967.

The Triumph. A Novel of Modern Diplomacy. Boston: Houghton Mifflin, 1968.

Indian Painting. With Randhawa. Boston: Houghton Mifflin, 1968.

Ambassador's Journal: A Personal Account of the Kennedy Years. Boston: Houghton Mifflin, 1969.

How To Get Out of Vietnam. New York: New American Library, 1967 (softcover pamphlet).

How To Control the Military. Garden City, New York: Doubleday and Company, 1969.
Who Needs the Democrats and What It Takes to Be Needed. New York: New American Library, 1970 (softcover pamphlet).
A Contemporary Guide to Economics, Peace and Laughter. Boston: Houghton Mifflin, 1971.
A China Passage. Boston: Houghton Mifflin, 1973.
Economics and the Public Purpose. Boston: Houghton Mifflin, 1973.

SECONDARY SOURCES

1. Books about Galbraith, in whole or in part

BREIT, W. and RANSOM R. L. *The Academic Scribblers.* New York: Holt, Rhinehart Winston, 1971. Discusses 12 Anglo-American economists from Marshall to the present. The chapter (about 30 pages) on Galbraith is well worth reading though the authors' sympathies toward Galbraith are lukewarm.
GRUCHY, ALLAN G. *Contemporary Economic Thought: The Contribution of Neo-Institutional Economics.* Clifton, New Jersey: Kelley, 1972. Discusses four contemporary heterodox economists and the goals of neo-institutional economics. Gruchy is probably the leading student of non-Marxist dissent. See index of this book for other comments on Gruchy's attitude.
HESSION, CHARLES H. *John Kenneth Galbraith and His Critics.* New York: New American Library, 1972. A friendly book, exhibiting conscientious scholarship. Devoted entirely to Galbraith.
SHARPE, MYRON E. *John Kenneth Galbraith and the Lower Economics.* White Plains: International Arts and Sciences Press, 1973. Devoted entirely to Galbraith. Really a long essay (86 pages) on Galbraith. The phrase, "lower economics" in Keynesian fashion, means "heterodox economics."

2. Articles by and about Galbraith

Most of Galbraith's more important articles manage to get collected and reprinted as books. The articles may appear under new titles but the titles of the books reveal very little; examples are *The Liberal Hour* and *A Contemporary Guide to Economics, Peace and Laughter.* Essays and articles not yet reprinted will probably appear in a new book soon.

Articles about Galbraith are legion. I list below a few of the more important ones.

GORDON, SCOTT. "The Close of the Galbraithian System." *Journal of Political Economy* (July-August, 1968), pp. 635 - 44.

MEADE, J. E. "Is the New Industrial State Inevitable?" *Economic Journal* (June, 1968), pp. 372 - 92.

SOLOW, ROBERT. "Son of Affluence." *Public Interest* (Fall, 1967), pp. 100 - 108. To this Galbraith replied with "Review of a Review," *Public Interest* (Fall, 1967), pp. 109 - 18.

Hearings before the Subcommittee of the Select Committee on Small Business, U.S. Senate, Planning, Regulation, and Competition, 96th Congress, 1st Session, Washington, D.C. June 29, 1967. This is not an article, obviously; it is an interesting record of a discussion between economists who reject Galbraith's views of the mature corporation and who have faith in an antitrust approach. Among these are: Walter Adams, Willard F. Mueller, and Donald F. Turner.

Two interviews with Galbraith reveal much about the man. They are to be found in: *Playboy,* June, 1968, and in the *New York Times Magazine,* Dec. 18, 1966.

Index